emotional
processing

emotional
processing

Healing through feeling

Dr Roger Baker

LION

A Lion Book
an imprint of
Lion Hudson plc
Wilkinson House, Jordan Hill Road,
Oxford OX2 8DR, England
www.lionhudson.com
ISBN 978 0 7459 5259 8

First edition 2007
10 9 8 7 6 5 4 3 2 1 0

Text Acknowledgments
pp. 19–20: Scripture quotations are taken from the New
Revised Standard Version published by HarperCollins
Publishers, copyright © 1989 by the Division of Christian
Education of the National Council of the Churches of Christ
in the USA, and are used by permission. All rights reserved.

Author's Note
I would like to thank the many patients whose experiences
during therapy are quoted in this book. The names and
personal details of all these people have been changed to
ensure the information is anonymous.

A catalogue record for this book is available
from the British Library

Typeset in 11/13 ITC Berkeley Oldstyle
Printed and bound in Wales by Creative Print and Design

This book has been printed on paper and board
independently certified as having been produced from
sustainable forests.

Contents

1   A New Understanding of Emotional Healing   7

PART I
THE SECRET LIFE OF THE EMOTIONS   17

2   Pure Reason   18

3   The Language of Two Worlds   27

4   Sixth Sense   37

PART II
EMOTIONAL PROCESSING: DISSOLVING
DISTRESS   49

5   The Emotional Immune System   50

6   Emotional Processing: Inside Out   58

PART III
HEALING THROUGH FEELING   73

7   The One Hard Fact in Psychology   74

8   Shell Shock   84

9   Battened Down and Bottled Up   95

PART IV
HOW TO SABOTAGE HEALING 107

10 Love and Pasta 108

11 A Pill for the Body, Soul and Spirit 120

12 Ruminating Your Life Away 132

13 Living in Harmony with Emotions 145

Appendix: The Idea Behind the Science 159

References 168

Index 173

1

A New Understanding of Emotional Healing

The kiss

'My mother held me by the hand and led me along the landing to the top of the stairs. I was so small my arm was at full stretch. It was mid-morning but the curtains were still closed and there was a strong, sickly smell of candles burning. She led me downstairs. On every shelf and every surface there were candles flickering. I'd never seen so many. The living room, where we two girls, my sister and I, usually played, was full of people sitting round in the shadows and mumbling to each other. I was led over to a box in the centre of the room. My mother picked me up to look into the box. I remember scraping my knees as she lifted me up.

'At first I couldn't understand what I was looking at. Flowers and some blacky-grey hair. Then I realized the hair belonged to my auntie. She was lying there, white and still. I didn't know what a corpse was, it was the first time I had seen one. Then I was being tilted forwards, actually towards this… dead body, and my lips were being lined up with the lips on the dead body, and I was being told, "Kiss… kiss your auntie."

'I must have let out an awful scream – I remember the shock of hearing my own scream – and I wriggled free and ran off to the kitchen. I was crying and gasping for breath, and had images of dead bodies and Aunt Claire which didn't seem to fit together. My mother rushed in after me, threw me across her knee and began to beat me repeatedly, shouting about "embarrassing her in front of the relatives… thinking only of myself… if you ever show me up again…" But the phrase that stuck most, I think, was "blabbing like a baby". After that I was dragged in again, lifted up much more forcibly this time and pushed forwards, despite my shivering and shaking, and made to kiss the corpse on the lips.'

It was getting darker outside the therapy office, and I walked across to the door to switch on the lights.

'And do you think this still has an effect on you so many years later?' I asked as I returned to my seat.

'It's hard to say,' Marjorie continued. 'I've sometimes wondered if the shock of that kiss… has somehow scarred me, but I can't quite figure out how.'

When Marjorie had first come to see me for psychological therapy she was not really sure what she was looking for. In the first session she tended to give minimal answers to questions and was obviously wary of seeing a clinical psychologist and scared of being regarded as a 'mental patient'. The appointment letter with the Department of Mental Health logo had not helped. Her GP had sent a brief referral letter to me mentioning that she had been depressed since the death of her father two years ago, that she was taking an antidepressant medication, and was generally having problems with relationships. He wrote:

'She is not the woman she used to be. She tells me she can't cope with life and has retreated to the safety of her house and mixes less with others than she did before. She doesn't really open up and it is hard to tell what is going on inside. She often smiles and is a pleasant and polite lady but I suspect this masks the depression she feels inside.'

This was our fourth session together. I had obviously 'passed the test' and she was prepared to open up and share more about herself. In the first session I had spent quite a lot of time explaining that she was not mentally ill, and that treatment by a clinical psychologist was not about 'curing mental disease' but helping her understand more about herself and her emotions.

I continued, 'Do you think much about the incident with kissing your auntie?'

'No, not really, this is the first time I've thought about it in… let's say two years.'

I recalled a moment earlier in the session when she had briefly looked sad, then suddenly sat up straight and composed. Just before she had referred to her father 'passing away' but had quickly changed the topic to more mundane matters, saying that was all behind her and she was no longer upset by his death. I felt that it would be useful to come back to this point

'Earlier in the session you were talking about the recent death of your father. You suggested it had not upset you at all.'

'That's right, not in the least,' she said.

'Do you mean you didn't love him, you didn't have much of a relationship?' I quizzed.

'No, no, no, that's not it,' she said, quite distraught. 'No, that's the thing. I loved him very much. I still do. But I can't…'

'Do you ever feel like crying?' I asked.

'I so much want to cry. People say you get a lot of relief from crying, a sort of still after the storm. But I never get that. I want to cry, I'd like to… but then along comes… a block.'

At this point in the session I thought it would be helpful for Marjorie to explore this 'block' in more detail, to understand it and to pin it down. So I pursued a line of questions helping her to explore exactly what this block was.

'What could you compare the feeling to?' I asked. At first she didn't understand what I was getting at, but after some explanation she was able to describe it.

9

'Like a huge black cloud that covers everything and muffles things.'

'I'd like you to just take a few minutes to look into that cloud and tell me more about it. Don't rush, take your time.'

After a long pause, she replied, 'It's a nasty feeling.'

'Of...?'

'Just nasty.'

'Is it like a feeling of depression?'

'No. Not depression. It's more like...' Marjorie seemed lost at this point. She was obviously struggling hard to identify what the feeling was.

'... guilt. Yes, I think it's guilt. A terrible black guilt.'

We sat in silence for a while. It was almost completely dark outside now, with a bit of a wind picking up.

'Tell me, Marjorie, do you think there is any connection between this guilt and what you told me about kissing your auntie?'

The silence was so very long at this point I half wondered if Marjorie had actually heard me, but I sensed that something important was happening.

Then I saw a wonderful thing. Small but wonderful. There was a tear running down her cheek.

Marjorie had learned as a child that it was wrong, very wrong indeed, to make a fuss, to cry or scream. The incident with her auntie's corpse had left a scar, just as she suspected it had, but there had been many other incidents in her upbringing in which crying and 'making a fuss' were scolded too. As became clear in later sessions, Marjorie not only had a blockage with tears but also with any lighter feeling such as joking, laughing or showing affection, even at the age of forty-six.

Before our session Marjorie knew she had a blockage in her life but she had not understood what it was all about. The session had helped her clarify that when she was about to experience tears and other emotions a 'black cloud' of guilt descended and blotted out her feelings. Also she had not seen how closely linked her emotional reactions were to experiences in her childhood. She had assumed that, because they were so many years ago, they no longer exerted any influence over her. She now realized that her childhood experiences had taught her that expressing feelings openly was selfish, childish, bad and an embarrassment to others. Over the next few sessions, as Marjorie began to reject this 'phony guilt' and allow herself to cry and show affection, she broke free of the emotional restraints that had blighted her life for many years.

Suppression

> 'To keep a stiff upper lip: Vb. keep calm, compose oneself, keep cool; master one's feelings, keep one's hair on; not turn a hair, not bat an eyelid; be patient, show restraint, forbear; put up with, stand, tolerate, bear, endure, support, suffer, abide; grin and bear it; brook, take it from, swallow, digest, stomach, pocket.'
> *Roget's Thesaurus*

The stiff upper lip belongs especially to Britain. The British are apparently renowned throughout the world for their mastery over the lip. But wait – what about Princess Di's funeral? What about the spontaneous outpouring of grief throughout the nation? Are the British stepping out of the repressive straightjacket of emotional control into a more healthy and open expression of feelings, or are they, as a nation, unable to control their impulses any more? Didn't the stiff upper lip serve the British empire well? Surely it did no harm? Wasn't society as a whole healthier? Or is it that people are just soft nowadays, having to indulgently express themselves at any cost?

Emotions are something of a mystery and they pose many questions. They are a power and a force that are not easily tamed. From falling in love to road rage, they often appear to have a life of their own. But is emotion important? Does it have any meaning or value in the twenty-first century? Or is it merely the expression of our primitive ancestry? Should much attention be paid to emotion or should it be assigned to the rubbish-heap of vestigial and unhelpful urges that evolution has unfortunately landed on mankind?

How is it best to live with emotions? Struggle with them; control them; calm them down; ignore, suppress, deny them? Some can live well enough with positive emotions but struggle with their negative feelings, such as anger, jealousy or anxiety. Others can even find pleasurable feelings, such as sexual desire and craving for unhealthy foods, alcohol and drugs, as much a problem. Is there a way of harnessing emotions, of living in harmony with them, or even of finding meaning and fulfilment through them?

Let it all out or keep it all in?

There is also the question of how feelings should be expressed. Are there healthy and unhealthy modes of expression? Are some South American nations right to regard the expression of anger as a sign of maturity in adolescent men, or should the Inuit people be preferred in thinking that temper should be reserved for young children and the immature? Of all the factors that have defined our identity in the twenty-first century – political, economic, technological – one little idea, one concept has, as it were, been burrowing quietly beneath the collective unconscious of the Western world and has shaped the view of healthy and unhealthy expression of emotions. In 1894, Sigmund Freud wrote a journal article in which he described for the first time the condition called 'anxiety neurosis'.[1] The idea of neurosis has been readily absorbed into Western thought since then, but that is not the most significant aspect of this article. Freud speculated that anxiety neurosis was primarily caused by a frustration in sexual arousal. A woman could develop anxiety neurosis if her husband broke off intercourse without satisfying her, and 'if, on the other hand, the husband waits for his wife's satisfaction, the coitus amounts to a normal one for her; but he will fall ill of "anxiety neurosis".' Freud's critics slated the article – if coitus interruptus (being a major form of birth control at that time) caused anxiety neurosis, then half the population should be struck down with it. Freud modified his position and over the years developed a much more subtle view of repressed sexual urges in the mental health realm. However, the germ of an idea was presented to the scientific community, and psychologists often refer to this as the 'hydraulic theory' of emotions.

The crux of Freud's idea at this early stage of his theorizing was that psychological energy is like water – flowing, bubbling up, moving. Crucial life events create a massive flow of new energy. If the flow is restricted, or blocked, pressure can build up and must find an outlet of some form or other. Likewise, restricting the flow of emotions and impulses is thought to be harmful, and may cause the flow of energy into other directions. In psychological terms, repressing, restricting or blocking important impulses and emotions can cause 'mental pressure to build up', so that energy is re-routed into mental symptoms or physical illness.

The popular press in Western societies overwhelmingly suggests that bottling up emotions is harmful, and that our feelings must be released, expressed in tears or anger, or we must share our soul with another person.

The writer Ruth Vose in her book *Agoraphobia* describes this very clearly as part of her recovery from this illness:

'As I gradually became more self aware, I noticed distinct correlations between my various physical and nervous symptoms. If I suppressed any aggression, I would get colitis, fear of cancer resulted in lumps, anger resulted in vomiting, repressed speech (fear of saying what I really felt) resulted in sore throats. I found that if I tackled the underlying problem (for

example, let my anger out rather than keep it in) the physical symptoms would automatically disappear.'[2]

The question is whether emotions are really like energy that can be restricted, or is this merely a metaphor that has been accepted as true?

This book is written for anyone who wants to understand more about emotions. I am a clinical psychologist, so the emphasis is on the healing of the emotions. It contains insights on how to come to terms with this often stubborn part of our make-up, drawing widely from experiences I have had with patients during psychological therapy.

But this book is about more than the healing of the emotions. It presents an in-depth account of a new psychological theory of emotional healing, called emotional processing. Many psychotherapists, counsellors, psychologists and neuro-psychologists refer to emotional processing as if it were a well-established field of knowledge. Although psychologist Jack Rachman introduced the concept of emotional processing in 1980, it has not developed much since then. Starting with my research in emotional processing and panic attacks in 1988, a research team has been built up to explore emotional processing in everyday life, psychological disorder, psychosomatic conditions and physical distress. We have developed a new theory, a new therapy and a new assessment, and we are collaborating in research with many centres across the world. You can read more about how the approach was developed in the Appendix, 'The Idea Behind the Science'. This provides some biographical details of how this area of research became significant to me, and how research that started with a *cognitive* approach to distress ended up as an *emotional* approach, and it provides a general background to emotional processing.

This book is the first time this ground-breaking body of research has been drawn together, making new insights available to a wider readership in non-technical language. It shows how an understanding of emotional processing can be useful in anything from everyday arguments, hassles and stress, to major psychological distress and trauma. Working with the body's natural emotional processing is so much easier than trying to contain and control what seems at times like a wild animal.

The book is structured in four parts. The first part, 'The Secret Life of the Emotions', gets to the root of one of the fundamental misunderstandings about emotions in Western culture, that emotions are a sort of primitive, hard-wired nuisance that get in the way of rationality and logic. This section presents a more integrated view of emotions and reason, which allows the amazing potential of our emotional system to be recognized.

The second part, 'Emotional Processing: Dissolving Distress', goes on to explain what emotional processing is; that we all possess a sort of second immune system, dedicated not to physical protection but protection from emotional hurt and trauma.

The third part, 'Healing through Feeling', is the hub of the emotional processing approach. With illustrations from four clinical cases of panic, phobias, alcoholism and trauma, the main psychological principles involved in emotional healing are explored.

Part Four, 'How to Sabotage Healing', is a manual of bad practice. Chapter 10, 'Love and Pasta', looks at the cultural determinants of attitudes to emotions, highlighting how negative 'emotion schemas' can enormously aggravate life's emotional distress and hurt, sending emotional processing into overdrive. Chapter 11, 'A Pill for the Body, Soul and Spirit', explores, through a close examination of psychological therapy for a patient suffering severe bodily pains, the problems of a somatic, or bodily, focus to emotions. Chapter 12, 'Ruminating Your Life Away', explains what happens when it is impossible to get emotional distress out of one's mind.

The final chapter, 'Living in Harmony with Emotions', draws together the various strands, and suggests how the emotional and rational sides of a person can work in harmony to produce the maximum benefits to health.

PART I

The Secret Life of the Emotions

2

Pure Reason

Reason over emotions

*Standing in the light of the crude window, Origenes Adamantias
(better known as Origen) studied the knife laid on the leather skin
before him. The shouts and noises of the great city of Alexandria
had lessened now that evening had come, but his mental
concentration was such that he was rarely distracted by noises, or
appetite, or discomfort.*

*Origen had developed a name as a 'great teacher' in the city.
Today he had broken his usual routine of teaching scripture to his
ardent students at the catechetical school, from which it was
possible to see the towers of the great library of Alexandria.
Paradoxically, this great centre of wisdom and knowledge was
separated by only a few streets from another great centre, the
amphitheatre, and it was from this district that Origen had just
returned. Around the amphitheatre were scores of small shops
where metal workers, braziers and swordsmiths worked. He had
sought out a smithy, lit by a great furnace within, to have the knife
sharpened. The leather skin was needed to wrap the blade, now too
sharp to be handled.*

*The knife had glinted for a moment in the light of the burning
brazier; it caught his eye and for some reason, he thought of his
father, tortured and killed for his faith. He remembered the letter he
had written to his father in prison, encouraging him and
strengthening his resolve to be a martyr, exhorting him to 'take heed*

not to change your mind on our account'. When his father had been
tortured and killed Origen had not allowed any sadness that might
deter him from his spiritual calling to take root in him. In his study
of the scriptures he had somehow become transfixed by the words of
Jesus from Matthew's Gospel, 'For there are eunuchs who have been
so from birth, and there are eunuchs who have been made eunuchs
by others, and there are eunuchs who have made themselves
eunuchs for the sake of the kingdom of heaven' (Matthew 19:12).
Although the context of these words was a discussion of marriage
and how one could serve God in an unmarried state, Origen had
seized on the literal idea of making himself a eunuch for the
kingdom of heaven's sake. To him, it represented the ultimate
sacrifice of the world and the flesh.

To understand how one of the great teachers of his time, a great
intellectual and early church father, could reach this conclusion
we need to explore Origen's views of reason and emotion. The
Stoic philosophers, spanning several centuries in Greek
thought, advocated *apatheia*, that is, the eradication of
emotion. The Stoic Crysippus viewed emotions as based on
false assumptions of things being 'good' or 'bad'. If one
reached the understanding that no event or external force can
be good or bad in itself, there is nothing to feel emotional
about. In Crysippus' view, right 'judgments' resulted in a lack
of emotions.

Origen brought a Stoical viewpoint to his Christian faith.
God, he argued, was pure reason, devoid of emotion. In the
same way, humans should rise above the sinful, fleshly,
emotional side of their nature to embrace pure intellectual
enlightenment, the higher side of their nature. He took from
the Stoics the idea of 'first movements', that is, there is a
tempting movement to start feeling the emotion proper – a sort
of pre-emotion – and that this must be resisted, so that no
emotion is felt. Origen referred to Jesus's prayer in the Garden
of Gethsemane before his impending arrest – 'He took with
him Peter and James and John, and began to be distressed and

agitated. And he said to them, "I am deeply grieved, even to death"' (Mark 14:33–34) – and argued that Jesus had experienced the first movement towards feeling sorrow, but being perfect he was able to resist this movement and not actually feel anything.

This view of the sinful nature of emotions and feelings and the imperative towards pure reason provides the background to understanding how, in AD 204, Origen picked up the knife and removed his own testicles.

Hierarchy of tears

Although this is an extreme example, the idea of the purity and superiority of reason and the baseness and unreliability of emotions has been alive over the centuries. Unfortunately it has also become intertwined with ideas of masculinity and femininity.

Throughout the ages men have been regarded as guided by reason, unswayed by feelings, and women to be motivated by emotions. Research confirms that women cry significantly more than men, notching up an average of two to five crying episodes a month.[1,2] Women do the job properly, too; men typically have tears welling up in their eyes, but women allow the tears to run down their cheeks. These rather arid statistics lend weight to the popular idea that women show their emotions more than men. But that in itself means little. The problem is that such differences that do exist have been used as evidence of the superiority of men over women. Medieval writers on 'generation' regarded men as the perfect version of humanity and women as flawed – as this summary of the writings of medieval authors reveals:

'The female form was a faulty version of the male, weaker, because menstruation and tearfulness displayed a watery, oozing physicality; female flesh was moister and flabbier, men were more muscular. A woman's body

was deficient in the vital heat, which allowed the male
to refine into semen the surplus blood which women
shed in menstruation; likewise, women produced milk
instead of semen. Women were leaky vessels,
menstruating, crying, lactating...'[3]

Ideas of emotionality, inferiority and femininity were bound
together for centuries in Western thought. In nineteenth-
century Britain the position had not substantially changed.

Something of this historical and cultural perspective is
implicit in Darwin's description of weeping in *The Expression of
the Emotions in Man and Animals*:

'With adults, especially of the male sex, weeping soon
ceases to be caused by, or to express, bodily pain. This
may be accounted for by its being thought weak and
unmanly by men, both of civilized and barbarous races,
to exhibit bodily pain by any outward sign. With this
exception, savages weep copiously from very slight
causes, of which fact Sir J. Lubbuck has collected
instances. A New Zealand chief 'cried like a child
because the sailors spoilt his favourite cloak by
powdering it with flour'. With the civilized nations of
Europe there is also much variation in the frequency of
weeping. Englishmen rarely cry, except under the
pressure of the acutest grief, whereas in some parts of
the Continent the men shed tears much more readily
and freely.

The insane give way to all their emotions, with little
or no restraint; and I am informed by Dr J. Crichton
Browne, that nothing is more characteristic of simple
melancholia, even in the male sex, than a tendency to
weep on the slightest occasions, or from no cause.'[4]

Darwin's implicit hierarchy of tearfulness seems to be
something like this:

1. The insane
2. Savages
3. Children
4. Continentals and English women
5. Englishmen.

The inferior little brain

The cultural backdrop associating emotions with inferiority, lack of control and lack of education (particularly in primitive peoples), set in contrast to rational thinking, formed the seedbed for the scientific development of the idea that emotions are primitive and are located in a 'primitive part of the brain'. In 1952 the neuroscientist Paul MacLean proposed that there existed an anatomical structure called the limbic system in the human brain that controlled emotional life.[5] He described it as a kind of primitive brain in its own right, separate from the neocortex or the 'thinking' brain. It was believed to receive inputs from the external world through sight, smell, hearing and so on, as well as sensations from the body. Its task was to integrate internal and external sensations, providing the basis of emotional experience. Although it was 'too primitive a brain to analyze language', it could:

> '… tie up symbolically a number of unrelated phenomena and at the same time lack the analyzing capacity of the word brain… might foolishly become involved in a variety of ridiculous correlations leading to phobias, obsessive-compulsive behaviour etc… [and] eludes the grasp of the intellect because its animalistic and primitive structure makes it impossible to communicate in verbal terms.'[6]

He assumed that the limbic system was virtually the same in the paleo-mammalian brain found in all lower animals. His proposal was that there was a primitive 'emotion' brain overlaid by a superior 'thinking' cortex.[7] This fundamental idea of an ancient–modern, paleo-mammalian–human, irrational–rational, lower–upper, inner–outer[a], smaller–larger[b], uncontrollable–controllable, brain persists today. How valid is this? Do we really possess an inner 'primitive' brain controlling emotion and a superior, larger, cortex controlling thinking, particularly verbal thought?

Joseph Le Doux, Professor of Science in the Centre for Neural Science at New York University, a leading neuroscientist, describes how the limbic system has survived as a concept for many years. He recognizes that the inner part of the brain is important in emotion, but the idea that the limbic system *constitutes* the entire emotional brain is, he argues, just not acceptable.[8,9] First, it is unclear what parts of the 'primitive' brain constitute the limbic system; second, while one structure, the amygdala, is related to emotions, other structures are not; for example, damage to the hippocampus, which is regarded as part of the limbic system, does not affect emotion but 'higher' thought processes such as factual learning and memory; thirdly, anatomists such as Harvey Karten and Glenn Northcutt were showing that so-called primitive creatures do in fact have areas that meet the structural and functional criteria of the neocortex. Animals might not think in terms of verbal logic, but are capable of cunning, understanding and memory, which do not belong primarily to the realm of emotional reactions. Le Doux proposes that the limbic system concept 'should be discarded'.

Antonio Damasio, Professor of Neurology and head of the Department of Neurology at the University of Iowa College of Medicine devoted chapters of his book *Descartes' Error*[10] to Phineas Gage, a hardworking, conscientious New England construction foreman, who lost a major section of his frontal

[a] the limbic system is proposed as located in the inner core of the brain
[b] the cortex of man is considerably larger than the proposed limbic system

23

cortex in a dynamite accident. He survived another thirteen years. All his rational faculties remained – memory, reasoning, speech, what MacLean called the 'word brain' – but aspects of his emotional life changed. He became 'fitful, irreverent, indulging at times in the grossest profanity which was not previously his custom, manifesting but little deference for his fellows, impatient of restraint or advice when it conflicted with his desires, devising many plans of future operation, which are no sooner arranged than they are abandoned'. He drifted from job to job, drinking and brawling, and died as much from neglect as from the epileptic convulsions that physically destroyed him.

Damasio argues that there are important areas of the cortex in man that are central to emotional functions, including the anterior cingulate cortex and somato-sensory cortex. He also examines the case of Elliot, a patient of his who suffered a tumour in his frontal cortex, which was successfully operated on. Elliot, an intelligent man with a high-profile job, like Phineas Gage, became unemployable as a result of emotional changes. The key point Damasio makes is that Elliot's memory and superior cognitive powers remained intact, and intellectually he had the ability to make the right decisions, yet he could not see any decision through, even finding it difficult to know what suit to wear, which route to travel to work, and what to eat – lamb or beef. Damasio argues that emotion, or an emotional decision-making ability, drives rational activities. Faced with many choices in life, some sort of emotional choice is necessary, or else, as in Elliot's case, one gets stuck in perpetual indecision.

Perfect unity

In the now famous book *Emotional Intelligence*,[11] Daniel Goleman takes up the position that Le Doux suggests is unsustainable, referring to our emotional life as 'hard-wired' in 'primitive centres' in our brain, as opposed to 'logical reasoning in the higher cortex'. This view of a primitive, hard-wired, inner core of the brain is popular amongst psychologists and neurologists and is strongly regarded as the accepted 'truth'. Richard S. Lazarus, Professor Emeritus at Berkeley University, who spearheaded research on the areas of stress, coping and appraisal, criticizes Goleman's position:

> 'It is not that we have two minds – one emotional and one reason – as Goleman has recently but unwisely put it when he wrote that 'in a very real sense, we have two minds, one that thinks and one that feels'. Nonsense. We have one mind, and it contains both thought and feeling. Passions and reason combine as one in our mind.'[12]

Damasio expresses something similar but at the neuro-anatomical rather than the psychological level of explanation when he says:

> 'I would like to propose that there is a particular region in the human brain where the systems concerned with emotions/feeling, attention and working memory interact so intimately that they constitute the source of energy of both external action (movement) and internal action (thought, animation, reasoning). This fountainhead region is the anterior cingulate cortex.'[13]

We must begin to think in terms of an amazing integration of emotion and intellect, which are inseparable. It is not an 'either-or' situation as both operate together in the human mind. Both are crucial and neither can operate properly without the other.

Psychologically and anatomically one cannot simply locate emotions in a primitive area of the brain, nor reason and logic simply in the 'advanced' cortex. To quote Le Doux:

'... as a result of these discoveries, it is no longer possible to say that some parts of the mammalian cortex were older than other parts. And once the distinction between old and new cortex breaks down, the whole concept of mammalian brain evolution is turned on its head. As a result, the evolutionary basis of the limbic lobe, rhinencephalon, visceral brain, and limbic system concepts has become suspect.'[14]

3

The Language of Two Worlds

The sleeper awakes

I open my eyes. Hazily scan a room. Lying on my back. Sucked into sleep again. Struggling… to awake. Tight eyelids. I force myself to look. A blur, a room. There is someone there. Sinking back into a dark, deep, sleep. I struggle once more to regain consciousness. There is a fear and a dread and unknowing. I do not know where I am, what has happened. I fight to stay awake. I drift in and out of consciousness many times, trying hard to stay conscious. As I peak above consciousness and open my eyes to see the room I am aware of a woman – a young woman – holding my hand. Wonderful! I hold tightly. I feel supported and secure. I need her so much, but she removes her hand and is gone. I sink back into oblivion. I struggle for what seems like many hours to regain consciousness, to get back to reality.

What was this? What does it describe? It took place in November 1980. I had had an operation – it was described to me as a minor operation – but the combination of anaesthetic drugs I had received had nearly killed me. It was my own fault – I had told the anaesthetist I was feeling sick and was afraid of vomiting. 'Yes, we can give you something special for that,' he reassured me. The 'something special' proved to be quite a cocktail of anaesthetic drugs. I have vague memories of something going wrong – of someone saying, 'He's going', the feeling of some sort of anxious activity during the operation. But the most significant part of the experience for me was the struggle to regain consciousness after the operation.

And the most significant part of the struggle was the touch, the hand held and what it conveyed. It was what I needed. I didn't know where I was, what had happened, even who I was. But I did know that touch was reality; touch was good; gentle touch was comforting; it meant that I was alive, awake, here. It conveyed a thousand positive things. It was what I needed at that moment.

Meaning is often regarded as being conveyed by language and the rules of reason and logic. Meaning is thought to be located in words and sentences – what a subject, verb and object tell us. But I could not comprehend words, sentences, reason. I was in a twilight zone somewhere between consciousness and unconsciousness where thinking, logic and reason played no part. However, the hand holding mine conveyed so many meanings, none of which are based on the language of words and logical meaning:

You're here.
You're OK.
I'm with you.
I'll look after you.
We're together.

They are based on a different system. A system with as much meaning but which had developed before I understood a single word. A system based on feeling, touch, love, relationship. Although I was barely conscious, I understood this as the nurse held my hand. I knew its meaning.

This illustrates quite well the fact that meaning can exist in different forms. The sort of meaning conveyed by words and grammar has a logical, structured basis. Touch and relationship also convey meaning but with a different structure, a different basis, a different set of symbols or building blocks. To put it in jargon, language and feelings are based on different symbolic code systems.

Dr Seymour Epstein, a senior psychologist at the University of Massachusetts, put this succinctly when he wrote:

> **'people apprehend reality by two conceptual systems that operate in parallel; an automatic, experiential system (emotions) and an analytic, rational system (thought), each operating by its own rules of inference'.**[1]

Wilma Bucci, Professor of Psychoanalysis at Adelphi University, has proposed a 'multiple code' theory of emotions that tries to unpick these different meaning systems.[2] She describes the verbal system as based on a code that has similar meaning for all individuals, which can be expressed in both verbal and written form. The verbal code is described as mainly a single channel, sequential processor, by which she means that we communicate or understand only one train of thought at a time, which unfolds progressively along a timeline. Language is mainly conscious, although there is much hidden or unconscious activity needed to support it, such as memory for words and implicit understanding of grammatical rules. Mathematics similarly shares a logical, single channel, sequential type of processing.

The non-verbal system could be seen as a multiple channel set-up that processes code from each of the senses, as well as from movement and bodily sensation, more or less simultaneously rather than in a single, segmental way, as with verbal processing. Like the verbal system, part of the code is symbolic, standing for features recognized equally by other people. But the non-verbal system also operates what Bucci calls a 'sub-symbolic' form in which one image does not stand for, or symbolize, something. In sub-symbolic processing, rapid, complex and automatic computations are performed unconsciously using implicit systematic rules of a different sort.

For instance, in walking, the hands, feet and body are automatically placed in the right position, and the rapidly changing visual scenes are calculated in what seems to be one seamless experience. It is a continuous, intuitive, multiple-channel system of processing.

The rational system, based on language, logic and reasoning, is laid down from about two years of age and onwards. It is consolidated and refined through talking to others, going to school, writing, study, thinking, taking in information, and formal learning (such as learning to read). The other system, the basis of emotions and feelings, is linked more closely to functions such as sight, touch, smell, hearing rhythms, pitch and melody, physical sensations in our body, sense of movement, balance and visual–spatial sense. This system contributes in a large way to the felt experience of self and is laid down early in life, some aspects even before birth. The Dr Seuss studies on human bonding by De Casper and colleagues show how pre-symbolic learning can begin even before birth.[3] Pregnant mothers were asked to read *The Cat in the Hat* to their unborn baby in the last trimester of pregnancy. After birth, babies showed a preference for hearing their mother read this familiar story than another Dr Seuss story. Familiar patterns of sound, intonation, timing and the general feeling it invoked could be recognized, although the babies could have no understanding of the meaning of the words themselves.

In its first six months the baby learns fundamental aspects of life, such as its mother's touch, eye contact with her, being suckled or fed, comforted, rocked, spoken to, soothed, played with. The baby is learning fundamental things about what a mother is, what another person is, what the world is like, closeness and bonding with another, and eye contact – the world of feeling and relating to others.

As you are reading this book, all the meanings and information coming to you are framed in a language structure and logic that we both share. My thoughts are transmitted in written words to you. This is very much the world of verbal symbolic code. Adults operate in this world every day, so much so that it is almost impossible to imagine what it is like to exist in a pre-verbal, pre-symbolic state. In looking back, all the concepts, ideas, beliefs and rules that structure life in the present act as a lens that may distort the view of the past.

Imagine a world not organized by language and logic, or by non-verbal signals and clear meanings, such as the concept of 'door', 'table', 'food', 'the-other-person', 'me', but a world fully experienced through impressions, feelings, touch, vision and sound. In this world there would be no sense of separately defined objects such as 'me' and 'other people' but a kaleidoscope of unstructured experiences. It is in this world that the experiential system, the basis of emotion, is laid down. Being close to a warm mother, suckling or being fed, comforting touch and being cared for, as well as pain, discomfort, overwhelming sights and sounds, are all part of this sense and feeling world. Mother's face and voice are recognized, eyes gradually learn to track mother's face, observe her gestures, mimic them, be stimulated by her cooing and talking, and to be relieved by her presence when wet, uncomfortable or hungry.

An everyday miracle

Ross had no plans that evening. Maybe he would chat with friends, perhaps have a drink in the pub and then go home to bed. But there seemed to be some other plan at work. He had met Avril earlier that evening to finish a work project they were both engaged on and simply, out of courtesy, he asked her along to meet his friends. He had no intentions towards Avril at all, but when he finally suggested they all go to the pub all his friends declined. He was bemused because the last thing they ever did was refuse a night at the pub. Were they setting him up? Was this destiny? He didn't know, but he could hardly go back on his word. So the two of them, Avril and Ross, went alone.

They ended up at The Angel at Symond's Yat, a rough sort

of place but with a roaring open fire in the centre of the room. They sat next to the fire, chatting away. Ross had noticed that Avril was physically attractive, but had put her in the mental compartment of 'not available', or perhaps he himself was not particularly available at that time. But as they chatted over a drink, in the light of the fire, he began to gain interest. He was surprised that she should want to be with him, that she seemed to be interested in him. He became more alert and noticed for the first time her flushed cheeks and beautiful eyes. He listened to her freely flowing conversation, her open sharing of thoughts and memories. He pricked up his attention and hung not just on her words but on the open, even childlike, way she shared with him. His attention focused right in on her eyes, her face, her mouth, her words. He liked everything he heard; he *really* liked all he heard; he was absorbed in her description of her life. She was talking about her family life and home – by this time he was very attentive and everything she said seemed somehow to reverberate with him. She started to talk about music in her family, how it was so much part of her life, orchestras, playing the piano from an early age, different pieces of music.

It was at this point that Ross suddenly, unexpectedly, without plan or intention, fell in love with her. A huge passionate power gripped him at the moment and wham – he was in love. Not a trickle, not a glimmer, not a gradual rising friendship or affection, but a sudden brick wall of love, absent one second and there the next. And it wasn't a frippery, a thing of the moment, a fancy. Neither was it sexual in a sensual sense. His love started then, continued steadily, took the knocks and blows over the years and persisted, and now, thirty years later, still remains. Ross and Avril married some years after they first met and are still together. How Avril moved from a vague acquaintance to whom he was extending a courtesy, to a loved-one in an instant of time is still a mystery to Ross. This was falling in love; it happened; it still has a pull and a power in his life today.

Love is all you need

The psychoanalyst H. Krystal[4] and the influential child psychologist John Bowlby,[5] regard love, closeness and attachment as fundamental emotions, laid down at this early stage. The psychologist Sue Gerhardt in *Why Love Matters: How Affection Shapes a Baby's Brain* goes one step further by claiming that love determines the neurological development of the brain.[6] If all goes well, bonding – the emotional attachment of mother and child, the feeling of oneness, closeness and love – will occur, and, according to a whole school of psychology (the object-relations psychologists), will become the primary template for all subsequent relationships. The scene for what happened to Ross and Avril was, according to attachment theorists, set many years before.

But attachment can go wrong. The psychoanalytical researcher Beatrice Beebe notes how, by matching and mimicking the timing and emotions of the mother, the baby recreates a similar emotional world in itself. In her laboratory, volunteer mothers had agreed for their interactions with their babies to be observed and monitored. Beebe describes certain mother–child relationships where 'derailment' rather than this bonding occurred:

> 'The usual long mutual (mother–infant) gazes with positive affect [the felt aspect of an emotion] were strikingly absent. Instead we observed complex and rapid sequences in which the mother 'chased' and the infant 'dodged'. The mother 'chased' by following the infant's head and body movements with her own head and body, pulling his arm, picking him to readjust his orientation, or attempting to force his head in her direction. The infant 'dodged' by moving back, ducking his head down, turning away, pulling his hair from her grasp, or by becoming limp or unresponsive… The mother's reactions to these 'dodges' were to become

sober, grimace, bite her lip, jut out her jaw or roughly
thrust the infant away from her. Towards the end of the
interaction, the infant increasingly lapsed into a limp,
motionless head hang.'[7]

I-love-you

The archetypal romantic relationship, I-love-you, is understood
as a relationship between two people. I, the lover, love her, the
loved one, or to put it in archaic prose, the beloved. The
beloved in turn is an individual who is also a lover, loves me,
which then makes me the beloved. Two individuals reciprocally
loving each other.

It would be easy to imagine maternal bonding as a similar
mutual relating of two individuals, because, physically speaking,
mother and child are separate biological individuals. But in the
experiential world of the child, this mutual sense of bonding
cannot be assumed, because the sense of 'I-ness' has not yet
developed in the child. In 1975 the psychoanalyst Margaret
Mahler wrote the influential work *The Psychological Birth of the
Human Infant*,[8] emphasizing that the psychological sense of
individuality was different and came later than biological
individuality. Through her observational studies of normal and
disturbed mother–child interactions, she concluded that babies
do not initially have a sense of themselves as a separate being
from their mother. So what do they have? Probably a world of
swirling senses without any clear distinction from mother; after
all, during pregnancy mother and child literally share one body
and, when born, mother becomes the main source for food,
soothing, comfort and touch. Bonding is unlikely to be the
mutual love of two individuals who know they are separate, but
a merged identity in which the baby experiences and absorbs its
mother's attitude and approach as if it was its own. If the baby
is loved, its feelings are diffused in love; if mother is cold or
ambivalent, it absorbs these emotions instead.

Mahler described a 'separation–individual' stage that occurs as the child is able to crawl or walk away from its mother. The child learns to tolerate separation from its mother and gradually develops a sense of being a separate individual. Other psychologists agree that a sense of individuality develops sometime after the child's biological separation from its mother, but disagree with Mahler on the importance of walking and crawling.[9] These powerful senses and emotions, the relationship with mother, whether healthy or disturbed, and the growing sense of self-identity all develop before language is mastered.

Grammar, verbal understanding and rational thought have not yet developed when these fundamental aspects of feeling, touch, emotion, relationship and sense of self are being laid down. If the experience and reality of those early years were of abandonment and lack of love, how hard it is with all the power of logical thinking to be persuaded that your friend/ partner/lover will not abandon you. The powerful, pre-verbal, pre-symbolic messages shriek out 'abandonment'.

It is not that the emotion system is more 'primitive' and is 'superseded' by a superior verbal–logic system, it is simply that in human development the emotion–feeling system is laid down earliest. It means that a different system with a different set of rules develops along with emotions, 'each of which apprehends reality by its own rules, and neither of which is more valid than the other. If either system defeats the other it also defeats itself, for they share the same body'.[10] Both systems grow and, given sufficient experience and stimulation, continue to be refined throughout life. It is not as if the emotion system suddenly stops developing when language begins, solidifying and marking time as an infantile system, while language and the rational system blossom and flourish. Emotions and cognition both develop together as mutually interacting systems. The two become fused as part of our total experience.

They are two worlds, existing side by side. It is not that one is good and the other bad, or that one is primitive and the other superior. They operate by different rules and principles. Mature

35

development is not learning to express one at the expense of the other; but rather learning to get a good balance between the two.

4

Sixth Sense

Extrasensory perception

It is not every day that a hairdryer falling from a great height drops into your bath and electrocutes you, but this is what happens to Nick Marshal, design executive at Sloane Curtis Advertising Company. It is also not every day that, when you recover consciousness, you are able to hear the thoughts of every woman on earth. On discovering his new-found power, Nick is at first terrified, but his analyst tells him: 'If men are from Mars and women are from Venus, and you speak Venutian, the world can be yours. You may be the luckiest man on earth. If you know what women want, you can rule.' And that is exactly what happens. Using information gained through his mental eavesdropping, Nick comes up with the best ideas at work, wins the contract, becomes the world's best kisser, becomes a responsible father, wins the heroine and generally changes from extreme macho chauvinist into sensitive 'new man'. Recognize the scenario? Yes, it's What Women Want, *the Hollywood film in which Mel Gibson's character demonstrates how the ability to hear the thoughts of others apparently makes humans into a kind of superman or superwoman, able to achieve anything. This was a twenty-first-century take on an idea popularized in the 1960s and 70s, when every advanced alien civilization in films such as* Zardoz *and* Beneath the Planet of the Apes *was advanced because they had extrasensory perception. ESP was a requisite for world domination.*

I can remember, as a new graduate, supervising undergraduate psychology students at Leeds University in 'ESP' experiments. This was cutting edge in the 1960s. A student sat in a booth looking at a special pack of cards with five symbols, transferring their thoughts by extrasensory perception to a partner sitting outside the booth. Their partner had to accurately perceive the 'vibes' and select the correct symbols. The object of this was really to teach students how to conduct psychological experiments and grapple with the crucial statistics that would usually demonstrate that the laws of chance were superior to the laws of extrasensory perception.

I wonder why so many science fiction films picked up on ESP? It seemed to self-evidently make humans into a superior race. Or could it? If you or I possessed a perfect version of ESP, would it really give us more information about our fellow human beings? It is an odd thing that thoughts should be glorified in this way – that knowing someone's thoughts helps you to know and understand their every motive; gives you absolute mastery over them; enables you to predict and be one step ahead of them every time.

The truth that has escaped the film-makers, and still eludes many, is that we do not need to acquire this superior power. We already possess ESP. But it is not ESP in the very mental, or cognitive, way portrayed by the cinema. The ESP we already possess is in the emotional experiential realm, a sort of *emotional* sensory perception. It is not magical, mysterious, supernatural or occult and we don't have to be an alien to achieve it. It is part of the emotional apparatus that all humans possess.

The good therapist

In 2001 Wilma Bucci wrote an important article explaining how 'emotional ESP' works in the psychotherapeutic relationship.[1] When patients come to a psychotherapist or counsellor for help, the referring doctor may have already sent a brief letter labelling the problem as 'social anxiety', 'depression', 'history of relationship problems' and so on, and the patients themselves may clearly express what they want changed. At the first session they may say, 'I've known for a long time...' or 'I have problems with the opposite sex – I'm not talking about casual relationships, but something wrong when it comes to commitment.' Or they may express their problems in terms of symptoms: 'I feel tense most of the time, I can't concentrate and I'm much more irritable with the family.' Or traumatic events: 'Ever since the mugging I've been a different person.'

However patients present their problems and whatever information they convey verbally, Bucci points out that there is a world of other information that reaches a psychotherapist: the way patients holds themselves, stand and move; and the way they speak – not the content, but features such as the pitch, timbre and volume of speech, speech rhythms, variations in emphasis and pausing – sometimes in harmony with the content of their conversation, but sometimes contradictory. All this carries crucial information about their problems and difficulties. Their eye contact, facial expressions, body posture and gestures all transmit meaning about the person. Although the therapist may consciously listen and try to understand what the person is saying he or she is also receiving and absorbing the 1,001 other messages the patient is transmitting. The therapist does not have to consciously take in these non-verbal clues. It is not as if therapists have to have a super computer as a brain, which consciously logs all the non-verbal stimuli. Most of these cues are picked up subconsciously and implicitly understood.

Bucci points to senses in the therapist such as hearing, sight, touch and smell as helping to provide the total picture of the patient's distress but is also open to the idea that 'senses beyond the reach of our consciousness', akin to the innate sense of direction in birds or realization of approaching danger in animals, may be operating without the psychotherapist's knowledge. All these complex cues and signals are absorbed and processed by the therapist to provide an overall sense of the other person and a sense of what is going wrong. Effective therapists are able to 'listen' to these feelings they have about the patient, so as to understand the nature of the patient's problems. They have the task of integrating the conscious verbal information they have heard from the patient with the many signals they pick up in the experiential realm. The therapist uses every part of the information the patient provides, verbal and non-verbal, to understand and then reflect back insights to the patient. This is why the disciplines of psychotherapy and counselling insist that therapists receive analysis before becoming practitioners; they can then correctly weed out their own unconscious material from that of the patients and focus on the patient's issues.

This process of receiving information from many sources, through felt experiences, trying to absorb, process and understand the felt experience and then consciously applying it, is not the sole ownership of a psychotherapist. It is a process that to some extent or another everyone can engage in. So much information is absorbed experientially from people other than through the conscious verbal content. It is necessary to learn how to access and interpret the experiential level. I am not referring to a management course on how to read body language, which is simply learning conscious classification of certain neat categories of behaviour, but rather 'tuning in' at the experiential level.

So Bucci has conveniently described to us, in the context of the psychotherapeutic relationship, how 'emotional extrasensory perception' works. Everyone has this ability; it is not magical, psychic or special. It is just being able to acknowledge and live with a more intuitive level of understanding.

Reading our bodies

The emotional experiential system is an amazing system giving us complex and subtle information about the interpersonal world around us. When it is working well, there is a stream of information that is first sensed, before it is consciously or verbally understood or organized.

The psychologist Eugene Gendlin fled from his home town, Vienna, in 1939, during the Nazi Third Reich, and with his wife settled in the US. He studied under Carl Rogers at Chicago University, where he later became Professor of Psychology and Philosophy. From a sound philosophical and psychological basis he developed a new approach to therapy called 'focusing'.[2] The technique is an incredibly simple yet powerful way to uncover problems by 'listening to' emotional experiences. As the word suggests it involves focusing – not just on emotions but on bodily feelings and sensations too. Gendlin refers to this as 'bodily-felt sense'.

The starting point might be an important life question, such as 'How is my life going right now?' In that context the person notes what sensations or emotions are stirred in their body. Their main task at this stage is simply to observe their feelings; to make no judgments or insights, simply objectively observe their feelings, their dimensions and qualities, rather like a surveyor might do when inspecting a house, impartially, factually. Having suspended judgment and categorization in order to note the raw data of the feelings, the second step is to try to put a description, a word, a phrase, an image, or a metaphor, to the observed feelings. A patient of mine recently declared that what he felt was like 'a long-distance run – you had to complete it, there were no breaks. Despite the grinding pain you had to continue.' The long-distance run described perfectly the gruelling nature of his experience. For him this metaphor came rather quickly but many may find a word or phrase that is adequate but doesn't really hit the nail on the head, and they progressively upgrade the phrase until the 'eureka' moment when the phrase perfectly fits with their experience. Gendlin describes how this 'clicking into place' can be emotionally releasing even though what the person realizes may be something unpalatable. The act of matching word to experience is a critical psychotherapeutic process, according to Gendlin.

Having properly pigeonholed the experience, the next question is 'What is this connected with, what does it relate to, in what way does my life feel like a long-distance run?' This ultimate phase can give insight into those issues in a person's life most deeply affecting them even though initially they had no inkling of their significance. They were barely acknowledged feelings. For those who have a good awareness of their own feelings, who are open to their experience, who are in tune with the emotional side of themselves, Gendlin's 'emotional focusing' may be self-evident. But for those who have not explored a particular situation greatly, it may be a powerful and focused technique.

I have not described focusing to explain a psychotherapeutic technique, but rather to pinpoint a truth. This is that, in the body, feelings, sensations and impulses are able to indicate what is most significant in life and where a problem lies *before* it has consciously been worked out. Although not initially aware what the problem is, there may be a sense that something is not right; it certainly has not been named, yet by emotional focusing the body can effectively be 'read'. It would seem that there are implicit and unconscious influences that may be causing distress, which, when interpreted, provide insight into life. Emotions and feelings in this case are a primary source of information that only later reaches consciousness and allows mental contemplation. The emotions, as it were, are the horse and the mental understanding is the cart.

Darkness

After my finals a group of us were invited to stay at a friend's cottage in a remote little village in Wales. We had been laughing and joking that evening but now it was late and we were getting tired and thinking about going to bed. As the conversation lulled, I was struck by the almost palpable silence surrounding the cottage. It seemed incredible not to hear the sound of traffic, people, or the background noise of the town. I went to the back door and walked outside to 'listen' to this silence. It was so different from the town, so pure, almost as if the silence had a sound of its own. Yet the purity was not complete; I heard a dog barking far away, and the hoot of an owl. Then, having stood outside for a while, I realized how completely dark it was. There is always some sort of glow in the town at night, but here, sooty blackness. I looked up. The sky seemed crammed full of stars, twinkling so much brighter than I remember back home. I stood amazed by the vast number of stars and their beauty. I did not contemplate how many million miles away they were, or how small we were in the totality of the universe. I just gazed upwards, speechless. How beautiful. How awe-inspiring. In and of themselves they seemed to possess beauty.

Now, many years later, I still stand and stare. But I know more now. As a clinical psychologist I have heard agoraphobic patients tell me how, as a child, they were gazing into the heavens and were seized by a fear of the distance and of infinity. They did not experience wonder, but dread. But back then, in Wales, as a student, I just looked at the heavens in awe and wonder.

This experience shows an important exception to what has been said so far. On this occasion there was no information to 'read' from another person. There was no other person, just the universe, out there. It was not interpersonal. There was no two-way interaction between two individuals. It was an objective and impersonal reality 'out there', not conscious, not able or attempting to communicate, that nevertheless stirred the emotions in a profound way.

Such experiences are not just related to the stars but to the sea, sunsets, vast or wonderful scenery, a sublime piece of music, ballet or a work of art. Even a mathematical solution or an 'elegant' chess move can be experienced as a beautiful thing. I won't say these things *speak* to us because they are impersonal, but there is something great, noble, harmonious or aesthetically pleasing that we respond to emotionally. Many of the emotion theorists of the last century have focused on emotions as interpersonal – one person's relationship with another person – but within us we have the capacity to appreciate beauty, truth and value in things that are not necessarily human.

Hearts of stone to hearts of flesh

It seems such a simple thing: that someone should touch an object and feel it as hot or cold, hard or soft, prickly or smooth. Yet what this amounts to is hard, impersonal, objective things out there in the world being transformed into the inner experience of a living being. We feel the rock with our fingers, which are covered with sensitive nerve endings that carry impulses up our arms to our spinal cord and brain. So far so good, it is similar to signals going down a telephone line. Now comes the impossible act of transformation. Those impulses are converted into the felt experience of a living being.

To convert the objective reality of the world out there into the inner felt experience I would have to say is impossible were it not for the fact that it actually happens. Perhaps because it is so everyday, we take it for granted. Although IT scientists have invented computers that model the processes of logical thinking found in humans, and even try to simulate the sort of scripts or schemas that people typically use to evaluate the emotional meaning of stimuli, the computer cannot simulate the simple miracle of feeling. It can act but not feel. Its actions are performed in response to a program, not in response to feelings. Human beings, on the other hand, act on the basis of felt experience. For instance, if food tastes unpleasant, it can be spat out (depending on the company!). This is not the same as a reflex, where the reaction, such as a knee jerk, is automatic. It is possible to hear, taste, feel and smell these sensations, to make sense of the felt experience and, if necessary, act.

If experiencing external reality through the senses was not impossible enough, now comes a far more impossible task: converting the world of relationships and meaning into felt experience. It is possible to experience important aspects of interpersonal or social environments, such as whether others are being critical, friendly, or respectful, and so on. We feel hurt if criticized, buoyed up if liked, have a sense of importance if respected. This does not just refer to single events, such as the boss being critical, but, as seen when looking at the 'good therapist' (earlier in this chapter), subtle myriad aspects of others' behaviour and demeanour can be emotionally experienced, so that the shifting patterns of interpersonal relations can be felt moment by moment. Just as physical senses can experience the physical temperature of water, emotional experience can pick up the psychological temperature of the surrounding world.

Through minute-by-minute emotional experience, it is possible to live, respond, relate, enjoy, contemplate and potentially experience a full life. Carl Rogers, the renowned American psychotherapist and founder of person-centred therapy, in encouraging the endeavour to 'become a person', said:

> 'It appears to be true that when a client is open to his experience, he comes to find his organism more trustworthy. He feels less fear of the emotional reactions which he has. There is a gradual growth of trust in, and even affection for the complex, rich, varied assortment of feelings and tendencies which exist in

him at the organic level. Consciousness, instead of being the watchman over a dangerous and unpredictable lot of impulses, of which few can be permitted to see the light of day, becomes the comfortable inhabitant of a society of impulses, satisfactorily self-governing when not fearfully guarded.'[3]

The mystery of the inner world of self

The 'self' is something of a puzzle and a mystery. It is the 'I' that experiences emotions, that feels anxious or experiences anger. How and why this 'I' experiences so many sensations and emotions is not clear. Also, why does this 'I' always feel like the familiar me? How is it that there is an inner sense of unity that does not change from day to day and often has not changed in a feeling sense since childhood? Many eighty- or ninety-year-olds say that although their body seems to be packing up in so many ways, they feel as if they are the same person inside as they were when younger. Why does it feel like me and not someone else? Why one me, rather than many? A popular view in psychology is that there are many selves operating differently in different circumstances, yet even if this is so, the 'felt me' has an unchanging quality about it.

Psychoanalyst Margaret Mahler's research suggests that the biological and psychological births of the individual are distinct. The organization of the inner world into a unified experiential self is not primarily a biological phenomenon but a psychological phenomenon.[4,5] Human beings can also contemplate the sense of being 'I' although the part that does the contemplation is still felt as the same 'I' as the part being contemplated. The sense of self is built on a foundation of experience and feelings, and elaborated emotionally and cognitively as life develops. It is the 'I' that experiences emotional hurt, emotional pain, happiness and joy. The emotions typically felt help people to understand what sort of person they are, what is important to them, what frustrates them, what their aspirations are, what drives them. Emotional experience helps them not only to relate to the natural world and to the interpersonal world of other people, but it also allows them to relate to self. A sense of self depends upon felt experience.

Emotional experience is the basis of the formation of relationships, the experience of the presence of others and of relating to them. It allows the receiving and giving of love. Emotions also allow the experience of aspects of the world that are beautiful, true, harmonious, awe-inspiring. They provide a glimpse of a greater dimension or sense of order.

By providing felt experience, emotions allow us to know the sort of person we are, what motivates and frustrates us. Emotions are an essential part of our identity. Lastly, and more basically, emotional feelings allow us to enjoy a range of activities, from simple physical aspects, such as food and drink, to more complex activities, such as being absorbed in the excitement and intellectual stimulation of a novel.

The same emotions that allow us to feel the positive aspects of self, others and the world could also allow us, if our life experience is cold or abusive, to experience a dysfunctional sense of self, alienation from others, and to feel that the world is cruel.

Good or bad, emotions help to make us human.

PART II

Emotional Processing: Dissolving Distress

5

The Emotional Immune System

Ogres turn to dust

Teenage daughters! Matthew had told his daughter the night before he had to attend an important meeting the next morning and could she make sure she was out of the bathroom by 7.30. 'Yes, of course, you don't have to tell me that.' Now, at 7.50, Matthew was rattling the door for the third time. 'Kerry, can you please let me come in? Now!' The mouthful of abuse he got from Kerry was just about the limit. Not only would he be late for the meeting and fail to make his presentation on time, but now he was being accused of being totally unreasonable. He was so angry he wanted to shout at his daughter but knew it would be counterproductive.

After finally getting washed and dressed, and without any breakfast, Matthew rushed to the car. He fumed as he drove at a dangerous speed to the office and in the meeting initially found it difficult to present his (somewhat delayed) presentation in quite his normal composed style. Yet now, driving home from work at the end of the day, he had quite forgotten the heated exchange of the morning and was feeling pretty benign towards his daughter as she described her part in the new school play. How had the ogre changed into a gentle giant?

In the first part of this book we explored emotions – how they are a crucial part of our being, and a vital and rich source of information about the world. The rest of this book concentrates on one of the transforming tasks of this emotional 'apparatus' referred to as 'emotional processing'. Life's progression of problems, dilemmas, conflicts, arguments, hassles, deadlines, tensions, losses and traumas ought to crush everyone, but somehow people largely manage to deal with and absorb troubles. 'For the most part, disturbing emotional experiences are satisfactorily absorbed,' said psychologist Jack Rachman when defining emotional processing in 1980.[1] This process of dissolving distress certainly refers to major life events, such as loss of a job, death of a loved one, or the breakdown of a love affair; but it also refers to the smaller daily events, including arguments, cars cutting in front of you, insolent shopkeepers, automatic answering services, and all those daily hassles the 'Grumpy Old Men' and '… Women' talk about on the BBC TV programme.

If there was no such process of dissolving distress, it would mean that every hurt, every argument, every aggravation, critical comment or rejection we have ever felt – from childhood through adolescence to adulthood – would simply accumulate, one on top of the other. It wouldn't just be that all past memories would fill the mind simultaneously, but so would the *affect* or arousal associated with each argument or hurt, culminating in an experience like a boiling cauldron of emotional pain.

Emotional processing refers to the process by which emotional disturbances are absorbed or decline, to the extent that they no longer bother or interfere with the normal experience of life. The signs of incomplete emotional processing include repeated or intrusive memories of the upsetting event, re-experiencing the original emotions, ruminative recycling of the event, poor sleep, nightmares, preoccupation with the event, poor concentration, tearfulness and a range of other experiences. All these suggest that the distressing event has not been properly integrated or absorbed.

In a lecture in 2003 I compared this natural process of absorption to the workings of the immune system: 'It's as if the body has a second immune system, an emotional system, devoted not to physical protection, but protection from emotional hurt and trauma.'

While medical science is developing a knowledge of the biological mechanisms involved in the immune network, involving antigens, antibodies, T-helper cells, T-killer cells, suppressor T cells, phagocytes and macrophages, is it possible to understand the psychological mechanisms that might be involved in the emotional immune system? The old adage 'time heals' gives the impression that there are no psychological processes at work to create this healing, just the simple passage of time. From the outside this appears to be the case with the physical immune system too. We catch a cold, time passes, and we recover. However, we now know that incredibly complex multiple biochemical processes underpin this apparently simple recovery. In general, for emotionally upsetting events, the emotional distress lessens over time. A broken romance hurts less as time goes by, tears and mourning after a death in the family eventually subside, and the psychological trauma of a car crash heals as the months and years pass. But is it actually the passing of time that brings this healing, or, as with the immune system, are there complex multiple psychological processes at work?[2]

Natural restoration

One such process is sleep. Going to bed, sleeping and dreaming, are part of a normal twenty-four-hour day, taking up about a third of a person's lifetime. The psychologist Wagner and colleagues at Lübeck and Cologne Universities gave research volunteers a number puzzle to solve that could be achieved either by hard mental slog or by gaining insight into a hidden rule that could dramatically speed up the problem solving.[3] In the group that had slept on the problem, twice as many had gained insight into the hidden rule as those resting during the day or those staying awake at night. Related research shows that sleep consolidates recent memories as well as inspiring insight.[4] Wagner concluded that 'sleep, by restructuring new memory representations, facilitates extraction of explicit knowledge and insightful behaviour'.

In this study it was not the passing of time that was the essential element in gaining insight, but the unconscious work done during sleep. It is not clear from Wagner's research whether it was sleeping or dreaming that was the essential element but whichever way, something that occurred during sleep facilitated insight. What works with simple mental puzzles should also help in the solving, restructuring and healing of life's everyday emotional problems, in the emotional processing of life events.

But there are many other activities, which, like sleep, may be responsible for the healing. In the rest of this book, one of the things I would like to explore is what are the psychological mechanisms underlying successful emotional processing – exactly how is distress dissolved? This is important, because it gives a better understanding of emotional experience and how correct emotional processing assists in coping more effectively with life's problems.

Disrupting the natural flow of emotional processing

Can the emotional immune system be disabled? John, a recovering alcoholic patient, who had experienced appalling sexual abuse throughout his childhood, discovered at fourteen that vodka diminished the pain and memories of the abuse and for the next thirty years lived in a perpetual alcoholic haze, consuming huge quantities of alcohol each day. A prison sentence at the age of forty-five enforced sobriety upon him, at which point he became overwhelmed by unresolved hurts and traumas from his childhood. Why was the emotional pain as severe at forty-five years as at fourteen years? Had the alcohol he had taken to numb the daily pain of his memories effectively put his emotional processing on hold? During upbringing children develop styles of handling emotions, some of which foster emotional processing but others that hinder it. Fortunately not too many children suffer as much as John, and so perhaps do not develop quite the extreme methods of dysfunctional coping that he did.

In the opening passage of this book we saw, in the conversation between Marjorie and me, how throughout her childhood Marjorie had learned that displays of emotion, positive or negative, were totally unacceptable and that this had formed a sort of 'block' to her ability to cope with emotional events later in her life. She was forty-four years old when her father died, yet she was unable to emotionally process the pain of his death because of this blockage. For her, this problem in dealing with emotional events not only affected her ability to grieve properly for her father, but it hindered her ability to deal with many of life's other stresses and hurts.

Is there a range of different ways in which emotional processing can be inhibited? John dampened his feelings through alcohol, whereas Marjorie had an unconscious block on her feelings. Do different methods of blocking emotional distress result in different patterns of symptoms? Or, to be more radical, could what we currently refer to as psychiatric disorders, such as depressive disorder, simply be the end result of a failure to process difficult emotional material? This is a second theme I shall explore later in this book. How can emotional processing be hindered and what effect does this have on us?

Mending broken hearts

Psychotherapy – the art of listening and helping patients understand their psychological distress – originated from a patient treated by Breuer, a colleague of Freud, called 'Anna O'. According to Freud, her problems originated from a time she was nursing her dying father, having already devoted much of her adult life to looking after him. His death represented a longed-for freedom for Anna O and she was excited at the prospect of her 'release'. But she could not admit this awful betrayal to herself. While caring for her father, Freud said, she had to 'suppress a strong excitement instead of giving vent to it by appropriate words and deeds', and, as a result of this suppression, she began to experience a range of neurotic symptoms. Anna O was helped by talking about her symptoms to Dr Breuer and she herself dubbed this 'my talking cure'.

Fascination with this case was an important factor in turning Freud from the use of hypnosis – his main treatment approach for those with psychological problems – to the 'cathartic method', the release of feelings through talking. He later developed this into a much more complex system of psychoanalytic therapy, but the 'talking cure' was born. Since this time (1910), scores of different psychotherapeutic methods have been constructed. Wikipedia provides an ever-growing 'list of psychotherapies' (well in excess of 100) and there are some even longer compendia of psychotherapies. Why does talking about emotional events bring help and healing to so many? What is it about the act of talking and being listened to that can transform a blockage like the one experienced by Marjorie into emotional release? And how does the relief of distress, which is the rule rather than the exception in psychotherapy and counselling, take place during therapy?[5,6]

So a further question this book seeks to explore is how psychological therapy operates to help reduce disabling and distressing emotional experiences. Are there a few basic processes at work? Are there commonalities between different psychotherapeutic methods? What can be taken from psychotherapy and applied effectively in everyday life?

Much information to help with the important question of how to live a healthier emotional life and prevent prolonged emotional distress will be gained from an understanding of:

- How emotional processing operates to reduce the experience of distress.
- The ways it is possible to inhibit or block this rather natural process of healing.
- How casualties of poor emotional processing can be rehabilitated through psychological therapy.

Ultimate suppression

'Then Jove's daughter Helen... drugged the wine with a herb that banishes all care, sorrow and ill humour. Whoever drinks wine thus drugged cannot shed a single tear all the rest of the day, not even though his father and mother both of them drop down dead, or he sees a brother or a son hewn in pieces before his very eyes.'
The Odyssey

Switching off emotional distress altogether is no answer. If, after the death of someone close, the pain could be removed, this would not be the same as emotional processing. In a way the emotional pain reflects the value placed on that which is lost – we grieve most for those we love most. Feeling no grief would almost be like negating our love. Gradually working through the pain can be both strengthening (developing the ability to cope with other problems) and creative (reaching towards new solutions and a new way of being), and the pain is like a worthy homage to the one who died (rather than a cheap gesture). In 'Body and Soul News' (*The Times*, 9 April 2005) I read an article that I found quite chilling. 'Making a Blank Canvas' reported at the Annual Cognitive Neuro-Science Society Conference on research into efforts to remove traumatic memories. Already antidepressant drugs such as Triptanol have been shown to stop memories becoming ingrained if taken within a few hours of a traumatic event, and another drug, Inderal, is now available online as a supposed post-trauma 'forget pill'. The article suggested that remedies for instant forgetting are not far away. What would it be like if it was just a matter of taking a pill after an upsetting event so that it was entirely forgotten? Could life be navigated by choosing what to remember and what to forget, thus constructing an altogether sweet and happy pathway?

The way in which difficult emotional events are processed has real benefits for coping in everyday life and possibly preventing more serious problems developing in the future. For instance, is it healthier to distract one's mind from a hurtful event or to think about it? Is there an optimal level for how much time one should think about painful memories? Does ruminating on an event simply exacerbate it or can it help resolve it? Should feelings always be expressed? Should the most powerful feelings be controlled? All these and many other issues make sense with a deeper understanding of emotional processing.

6

Emotional Processing: Inside Out

The elements of emotion

'I don't feel I am an emotional person and when you first said about emotional experience, I thought, "I don't have any." I don't focus on emotions a lot. I just accept that's part of things and almost get on with things.'

Susan's initial response was not encouraging. She had come as a volunteer for a research study in which she would be asked to talk about a recent positive emotional experience and then a negative experience. Susan, a teacher at a private school, found it difficult at first to reflect even on the positive side of her emotional life, but with an effort she did speak about her feelings, and eventually shared her negative experiences too. For her, emotions were an uncharted territory, rather unpleasant, to be avoided rather than embraced.

In this chapter I would like to look at things that Susan would have preferred not to look at; to explore the dynamics of emotions and to look more closely at emotional experience and what lies behind it. I would like to unpack emotional experience and try to describe its different components in order to understand better how emotional processing works. It is a bit like taking an engine apart and laying all the parts out on a garage floor. The real living whole is of course more than the sum of its parts, but the exercise does help demonstrate what emotional life consists of, how emotions operate and how things go wrong in handling emotional issues.[1,2,3,4,5] To make the 'deconstruction' clearer, this chapter includes a series of diagrams that are developed in a later chapter, showing the model of the different elements of emotion.

Emotional processing starts with an event, usually something unpleasant, that somehow we are able to accommodate, absorb, or deal with. In Susan's case, she was quick to identify what the event was. She began by saying, 'I can tell you I've been seething all the way here.' She had travelled by car from her school at Southampton to Bournemouth University, where Professor Les Todres and I were conducting the research interviews.

'Seething all the way?' asked Les.

'Yes,' she replied.

'That's a good place to start,' he concluded. So that's just what Susan did.

'Just a bit of background, then. As you know I'm a senior teacher working in a large private school near Southampton. I assist the headmistress. What made me so cross today is I often feel like piggy in the middle between her and other people.

'She will suddenly tell you to do things. For example, last week she had an email from a person wanting to come down to meet to discuss a timetable management system with her, myself and two other people. She just said to me "Arrange it for such a date" so I sent three letters off to the other people myself using my email, even though she's got email too. And she came to me this morning and this person has replied to her, saying that he was coming on one of the dates. But she just said, "That's no good, I can't do it."

'So I was seething because that made me feel devalued as a person. I feel I've been ignored, left to make arrangements, and yet things are out of my hands, so why should I bother? So that's the setting of it.'

'Is it OK to talk further about that one?' Les asked, aware that the information might be quite sensitive.

'Yes. It will probably help.'

Next, Les tried to get to the heart of what Susan had experienced.

'Like before, we are going to try to slow down the experience again. Could you help me understand the moment in which you became angry? Is it angry? You said "seething". Could you help me understand that moment? Could you talk me through that?'

'I can't remember what I was doing now. I was just doing something in the office. I can't remember how I was feeling, but obviously just normal and OK. Then she came in and just said, "I've had an email. The eighth is no good for me. Rearrange it," or something like that.'

'And then what?'

'Immediately it seemed that something rose up within me and I felt very angry, because (a) I'd been left to do it, and I had done it and now it wasn't convenient, and (b) that although I had contacted this person, she had replied to Sharon [the headmistress]. I checked to see whether I had a copy of the reply and I didn't. That made me feel just like piggy in the middle, unimportant, devalued.'

'There's quite a lot in that so we will focus on that for a moment. The first thing you said was this feeling of rising up. Could you describe that to me? What is that feeling of rising up?'

'It was physical, definitely physical. From my stomach, something coming up, but it was emotional as well. It seemed to be a physical thing. I think I actually felt a bit wobbly in my stomach and I felt physical symptoms from that as well.'

'So something arose in you, you were aware of "being piggy in the middle", asking, "Why didn't she consult me?" The other word you used was "ignored" and you also used the word "seething". Could you help me understand the word "seething"?'

'It was just as though something had exploded within me. I

was perfectly OK one minute and as though one word, one sentence could do something within me that seemed to be like an explosion. Something being released, something bubbling up.'

This real human experience shows how complex emotions can be. The classical division of 'universal' human emotions into six different types found in many psychology textbooks – anger, disgust, fear, joy, sadness and surprise – seems too crude. What we see with Susan is a complex interpersonal situation that carried many meanings for her, resulting in a kaleidoscope of thoughts and feelings.

Registering the emotion

The event that had made her 'seethe all the way' to the interview was not totally straightforward. Her boss had asked her to arrange a date for a meeting. The boss could have done it herself in the first place, but had asked her to do it and then rearrange it when she found it did not suit her. It is not so much the stark events that stand out, but the subtle meanings Susan attributed to them. No doubt these meanings were based on the way Sharon, the headmistress, had behaved in the past, and Susan's knowledge of Sharon's personality, but she read this as being treated as 'piggy in the middle' (caught in a situation over which you have no control), 'unimportant' (Sharon is important and powerful, I am insignificant and subservient), 'devalued' (it's as if my actions were useless).

Figure 1 (see page 62) shows the first part of the 'Model of Emotion' in which the '**input event**' is crucial. What in the model we rather dryly call 'an input event', actually consists of an event (a hard fact that could be caught on camera) *interpreted* by Susan in a particular way. Her interpretation of 'piggy in the middle, unimportant, devalued', was instantaneous, subconscious, personal, based on her knowledge of Sharon, and on her own personal values, needs and weaknesses. In films, situations are often presented in black and white. For example, Sharon was unreasonable/Susan got hurt. But Susan's emotional reaction was not the direct result of Sharon's behaviour. It was caused by her understanding or interpretation of her behaviour or, in psychology-speak, her 'cognitive appraisal'. She might have been correct in her appraisal or she might have been incorrect. Either way it makes no difference to the emotions she felt. If something is appraised as unfair, unjust, demeaning, then the person will feel hurt regardless of the truth of their appraisal.[6,7,8,9]

Figure 1: Registering the emotion

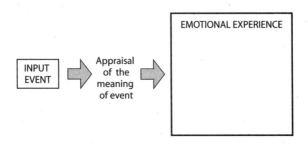

Experiencing the emotion

The emotions Susan felt stemmed directly from her reading of the situation. She felt a physical sensation rising up from her stomach, which she called 'seething', as if something had been released or an explosion had occurred within her.

Susan described her experience in terms of both bodily sensations and emotional feelings. An idea of an 'explosion bubbling up and something being released' suggests a process or a dynamic movement that could be emotional or physical. Figure 2 shows the addition of the **emotional experience** element of emotions.

Figure 2: Experiencing emotion

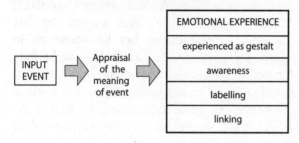

Emotions and physical sensations are inseparable.[10] It is hard to imagine an emotion without a physical side to it, although it is easy to imagine a physical sensation without an emotion, such as having an itchy foot.

An emotional experience also has a *psychological meaning*.[11,12] Susan was seething, hurt, feeling used, unimportant. She was a senior teacher but she felt humiliated because she was treated like a skivvy, an underling. In the early 1900s the German word 'Gestalt' was used initially to define a whole movement in experimental psychology and later a new psychotherapeutic movement in the USA. It means 'a whole', 'a completeness', 'a unity'; that the meaning of an event is all wrapped up in one parcel. And that is the essence of emotional experience – assuming there is normal emotional development during childhood – that the psychological meaning of an emotion is felt as a whole, as a unity. So for Susan, her perceived humiliation resulted in the seething feeling, being hurt, being taken advantage of. The psychological meaning is *felt*, along with the somatic components of the feeling. For instance, it would be unusual to say, 'I was clenching my teeth. My blood pressure seemed sky high. I was incredibly tense. I was banging my fists on the table and shouting.' It is usually felt as one entity – 'I was angry'.

This describes the physiological and behavioural elements that contribute to the total experience, but the psychological felt meaning is 'anger'. And anger does not hang in the air, experienced for no reason. The feeling of anger is the direct result of things said and done to the person that are appraised (correctly or incorrectly) as insulting, a snub or a put-down.

In writing the above I was reluctant to say the words 'normal emotional development', but actually there are quite a number of individuals who do not feel the Gestalt of an emotion, the psychological meaning, but instead concentrate on the somatic components that make up emotions. Their boss shouts at them at work and they continue working. Some time later they go to the coffee machine for a short break and realize they are shaking, sweating, tense and gripping the coffee cup so hard it nearly bursts. Yet they have not identified this as 'anger'; they have not linked it to their boss's unreasonable outburst. Actually they do not tend to think about emotions at all. Instead, they are on a 'somatic' plane. They say, 'I'm shaking, I'm hot, I'm feeling unwell... I must have caught that new flu bug they were talking about.' At lunchtime they take two pain killers, ring the doctor, make an appointment and hope their illness can be diagnosed properly. Here something has gone badly wrong: the person has concentrated on the somatic elements of their emotions, and missed the essential *meaning* of their emotions, and with it failed to identify the cause – the boss, or should I say, 'their appraisal of the boss'.[13]

Being able to experience emotions, label them and link them to causative events are elements of normal emotional experience.

Expressing the emotion

I have talked about 'an input event', 'cognitive appraisal' of the event, and of the emotional experience that follows. A third and crucial part is what the person does about it, what actions follow. Figure 3 adds the **emotional expression** element of emotion. Many writers on emotion refer to a natural and inevitable drive that individuals have towards outwardly expressing their emotions.[14]

Figure 3: Expressing emotions

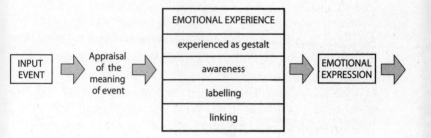

Professor Todres and I asked Susan to try to tell us how the feeling of 'seething' might lead to emotional expression.

'So all these things are happening in the seething?'

'Yes.'

'Could you talk us through that? How long did you sit there for? What happened?'

'I think I went back to what I was doing, but not fully concentrating because of all the thoughts that were going on. I think I did try to return to what I was doing.'

'You tried to return to what you were doing but some of those thoughts continued?'

'Yes. Probably only 50 per cent concentration was going into what I should have been doing. The rest was all a mass of thinking and emotions and seething still.'

'Was it going anywhere or just repeating itself?'

'No, it was repeating itself.'

'You didn't come up with any outcome or any decisions?'

'No.'

'So you started doing something else?'

'Yes. I think it came and went a bit like the other ones I was saying. But driving here, because my mind was able to float about different things, it was going over and over in my mind.'

'What sort of thoughts?'

'Again, just repeating all the things about "why bother?" I

suppose making some sort of sense how I tackle what I am going to do, because I've made no decision as yet as to what I am going to do.'

'That's interesting. So in the car you started making plans. You didn't start making plans earlier?'

'No. I thought, "I'm not going to think about this now."'

'Was that a conscious decision?'

'I think it's all a part of how I do deal with emotion, and thinking, "I'll decide this later" or "I'll deal with this."'

'It's a particular kind of putting the lid on, because you're not saying, "I'm going to put this out of my head forever." You say, "I'm going to deal with this later," there was an awareness in you that you would need to come back to it?'

'Yes. I suppose I needed time not to rush into making the wrong decision. It's obviously got to be a rational one. I've got to do something about it but I didn't want it to be made out of all the emotions there. I need to take a sideward step and think it through logically. It won't take me long to do, but I wouldn't have dealt with it there and then.'

'Why not?'

'Good point. I don't know, I think I wanted time to think it through and to do it at a time when I wasn't feeling so emotional about it.'

'So you sorted out what you were going to do, what you weren't going to do and where you stood in the whole thing? That didn't involve talking to Sharon, it was just about how to get on.'

'The practical side again.'

'How to move forward?'

'Yes. I wouldn't say to anyone about the good things. I also wouldn't talk to people about my bad emotions as it were, these type of emotions.'

'No one at all?'

'Very few people.'

'Even people close to you?'

'I'm always being told I don't talk enough about this sort of thing by my husband.'

'So do you somehow have to process it yourself?'

'Yes, I deal with it.'

'But you don't feel you have dealt with it now?'

'No, I don't.'

'So where are you with it now?'

'It's still going around in my mind. It will get dealt with when I get back and then most of the time it will be done and finished with, but it will come back at different times. Something else will trigger it off and it will come back again, so it won't have been completely dealt with, I know that.'

Not everybody shows such a controlled method of handling emotions as Susan. Emotion can be expressed directly in crying, laughing, telling someone what you think, shouting or even hitting out.[15,16] But it's not that simple. Some of these types of expression have an impact on other people, who change their behaviour as a result. A torrent of abuse directed towards the person who harmed you may get a torrent of abuse in return.

Susan used the 'back burner' approach of expression – 'I'll deal with it later.' This sort of approach ensures that the response is not in the heat of the moment. It is a sort of version of counting to ten when you see red, except it is counting to one hundred-thousand! Susan would come back to it later. In a way there is sense in this because it utilizes the 'incubation effect'. The most classic example of this is the renowned chemist August Kekulé, who spent months of fruitless research trying to understand the molecular structure of the chemical benzene before taking a break from his work. It was then that he made a breakthrough:

'I was sitting writing in my textbook, but the work did not progress; my thoughts were elsewhere. I turned my chair to the fire and dozed. Again the atoms were gambolling before my eyes. This time the smaller groups kept modestly in the background. My mental eye, rendered more acute by the repeated visions of the kind, could now distinguish larger structures of manifold configuration; long rows sometimes more closely fitted together all twining and twisting in snake-like motion. But look! What was that? One of the snakes had seized hold of its own tail, and the form whirled mockingly before my eyes. As if by a flash of lightning I awoke; and this time spent the rest of the night working out the hypothesis.'

It was from the sight of a snake holding its own tail that Kekulé was able to understand the ring structure of benzene. His mental strivings and thoughts needed an 'incubation' period, an unconscious sifting of data, before the solution presented itself in the form of a dream. For Susan the solution may not be so dramatic, but in the cooling-off period it is likely that some constructive solutions might emerge. Although this sort of delayed expression might be very sensible and rational, it is hardly a direct expression of emotions and would not carry the cathartic relief of an angry outburst, tears or a good moan to friends.

Emotions can be expressed directly, for instance, by arguing or talking to the person responsible for the hurt; or they can be expressed indirectly, perhaps by kicking the door or denigrating the person behind their back. They can be expressed verbally, such as by sharing the feeling with friends, using an internet chat room, talking to oneself about it, prayer (talking to God about it or expressing it to him), or writing it down. An emotion can also be expressed in action, such as playing a musical instrument, dancing, or painting, which express the issue in a direct way, or in other, more generalized, types of expression such as sport.[17]

The expression can be constructive, such as attempting to resolve matters with the 'perpetrator', asserting your point of view, thinking it through, getting guidance from others about what to do; it may be destructive, such as shouting or swearing at others, or hitting them; or it may be self-defeating, such as driving too fast, cutting oneself, or taking an overdose.

Regulating the emotion

Although the sequence input–experience–expression is a natural progression, individuals develop types of control or regulation of emotions throughout their life. Some types of regulation, such as not hitting others when angry, are helpful and generally lend to better integration with others; but some are harmful, such as controlling any outward sign of emotion, even tears. Figure 4 adds the control dimension, incorporating all four elements of the model: registering, experiencing, expressing and regulating the emotions.

Figure 4: Control of emotions

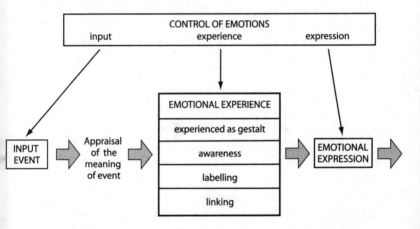

The control or regulation of emotion is part of a healthy childhood development, and the ideal is neither too controlled (for your own health) or too uncontrolled (for the health of others). In an ideal world it is 'just right'. But what is just right? Different cultures have different boundaries for what is acceptable, and there is not really a right answer. Many of us get it wrong. Some are unhappy because they feel altogether too repressed, too controlled; others are unhappy because they flew off the handle once again and hurt those they love, bitterly regretting the unkind words they uttered yesterday, words that can never quite be taken back.[18,19]

Control can occur at different stages of the emotional sequence.[20] Control or regulation might be at the 'input' stage, where the person tries to avoid any upsetting events, even just seeing them, for example, avoiding the sight of violence on the TV. This could involve avoiding challenge, change or specific situations, such as public speaking or going to the dentist.[21] Medical phobias are thought to be quite common although these are almost impossible to research. Avoidance of doctors and hospitals may not be too problematic until a life-threatening condition occurs. One sad newspaper article reported on a man with a phobia of hospitals. He developed a serious stomach problem and attempted to operate on his own; he died as a result. Controlling input is not all bad, though; avoiding dangerous situations, fights and problematic relationships may be quite healthy. It can be quite an advanced skill to change the 'input event', for example, persuading an irate colleague to calm down and thereby reducing the stress on you. This refers to controlling the input or originating stimulus for the emotion. But what of the regulation of the emotional experience itself?

Controlling emotional experience can be problematic. Whenever certain emotions, such as anger or unhappiness, are felt, some individuals attempt to squash, stifle or stop the feeling. They may become so good at this that they learn to stop feelings almost before they are consciously registered. Dissociation is such a complete cutting off of memories and emotional experiences that the person becomes emotionally numb or feels that their emotions are blunted, dull or blanked off. This can occur automatically as a sort of numbing protection after trauma, abuse, disasters or deaths in the family.

Controlling the *experience* of emotions is generally more harmful than controlling the *expression* of emotions.

This description outlines the model of emotions behind emotional processing. When we pat a dog and see it wag its tail, we have a perfect picture of an input (patting) and the expression (tail wagging), but absolutely no idea what happens in between. Does the dog feel happy? Can it control its feelings and their expression? It is this inner aspect of emotional experience, which we can only guess at with animals, that I have tried to describe and categorize in this model.

In Part III, I would like to breathe life into this formal psychological model by looking in more detail at the emotional experiences of patients during psychological therapy. These experiences all seem to converge on one single important element essential for the healing of emotional distress.

PART III

Healing through Feeling

7

The One Hard Fact in Psychology

Facing the demon drink

In late summer the evening light, the 'gloamin', seems to last for hours. It had been the perfect day at Balmedie, continuous sunshine yet with a pleasant chilling breeze that came in from the North Sea. A small group of men had gathered at the start of the day to help with the cutting of the hay, and Alex, at the end of the summer holiday, was with them. He was fourteen.

'When we had finished our work at the end of the day,' Alex recalled, 'a tray was brought out and we were all given a tumbler of whisky. The smell of the mown hay, the warmth of the evening, the satisfaction of working with the men, has always been associated with the first time I ever drank whisky.' This wonderful memory was saddened by the fact that Alex, now thirty-eight, was sitting in my office for our first session of therapy to help overcome the alcohol problems that had lost him his job, his house and nearly his marriage. The other poignant sadness was that the tray of whisky had been given to the men by the local church minister, a well-meaning gesture at the end of the day for hard-working men. The minister would have been mortified to see how that bright-eyed lad had changed into this tearful, haunted man.

It had been one of the first therapy cases I had been assigned when I started as a senior clinical psychologist at Aberdeen. It was not long after aversion therapy – associating drinking with drugs that induced vomiting, or with electric shocks – had ceased to become the dominant psychological treatment for alcoholism. After aversion therapy there were no standard clinical psychology treatment packages for alcoholism, so I had to devise my own approach based on the behavioural analysis model in which I had been trained. After a thorough 'behavioural analysis' of Alex's case, I decided to try an approach in which the 'antecedent stimuli' (the events that triggered drinking) would be presented to Alex without the 'reinforcing event' (the pleasure of drinking alcohol). I was to get quite a surprise from the results.

I needed, of course, to purchase the central 'antecedent stimulus', but since there are plenty of off-licences in Aberdeen, that was not a problem. There were even no eyebrows raised for an NHS purchase of a quarter bottle of whisky and a quarter bottle of vodka. After explaining the rather implausible approach to Alex – 'You sit in front of the whisky doing nothing' – he agreed to try it, but I think was somewhat sceptical of the mad English psychologist he had been assigned. I put the unopened quarter bottle of whisky on a chair, eight feet from Alex, and told him to simply look at it, in silence, while every minute I would ask him to rate his desire for a drink on a ten-point scale of severity. (Notice how 'scientific' this was!) What happened next surprised us both.

Almost as soon as Alex saw the unopened bottle, even without any whisky smell, he began to shake visibly and uncontrollably. His stomach turned over. He did not experience the desire to drink, just an overwhelming physical reaction. Over each successive minute thereafter he calmed down and shook somewhat less until after about ten minutes he felt no strong reaction. The next exercise was to bring the bottle closer (four feet) and repeat the exercise. Again there was an initial 'shock' reaction but it subsided quicker than on the first 'trial'. Next it was eight feet away with the bottle open, then eight feet away with the whisky poured into a tumbler. It was at this point that Alex told me about his first whisky in the evening sunshine at Balmedie.

Over the next few weeks Alex was exposed to a variety of alcohol 'stimuli', all moving towards realistic everyday situations. When he had to hold the whisky and sniff it continuously for five minutes he reported feeling nauseous with a revulsion to the whisky. He was able to repeat this for the next, most testing, trial, which was for me to leave him alone in my office with the whisky under his nose for ten minutes. When I returned he said he had not been tempted to drink. It was not that he was gritting his teeth and exercising his utmost willpower not to drink, but he did not *want* to drink. There was no desire left. These new experiences had fortunately cast a blanket over that memory of his glorious first whisky in the hay fields. He was reluctant to try some of the homework exercises I asked of him, such as walking into a bar where he knew no one and staying there for forty-five minutes (with a soft drink), but he succeeded in each exercise, until he felt his confidence and self-control were such that he had cracked the problem and that he only required 'follow up' sessions. Alex went on to put his life together, with alcohol playing only a minor part in that new life.

This therapy did not seem to work so much on strengthening his willpower not to drink, but more on removing the emotional desire for a drink. While we referred to this as 'behavioural therapy', the crux of the therapy was not behavioural at all; it seemed to have its impact on wanting, craving and desire – the emotional engine that drove Alex's behaviour. I did not see it as an emotional therapy at that time, though.

For phobias, the easiest therapy in the book

To get a fuller understanding of how psychological therapy has its effect on emotional healing we need to go 'back in time', back to an era preceding the emergence of behaviour therapy, to an era when there were no psychological therapies for specific conditions like phobias, obsessive-compulsive disorder or post-traumatic stress disorder.

In the mid-1920s, a Professor of English at the University of Wisconsin, William Ellery Leonard, who had tried several different approaches to overcome his agoraphobia, all without success, decided, along with his psychology colleagues, to really get to the bottom of his phobia, to crack it forever. He would use himself as the guinea pig. With his colleagues he would try to piece together as total a picture of his memories and experiences as possible in order to track down when and how his phobia started. He tried to make his system of memory recall as systematic and complete as possible, cross-checking memories with verifiable information where possible, adhering to proper standards of reporting, and involving objective observation and scrutiny of his data with his psychology colleagues. Leonard claimed that the book that resulted from this, *The Locomotive God*,[1] was the most accurate autobiography ever written. He managed to track the start of his phobia down to a specific childhood experience. While on a railway station with his mother at the age of three he was startled by a huge, noisy locomotive rushing past. Despite being able to track how this event set off a range of problems, he was still unable to overcome the agoraphobia and had, sadly, to settle for a severely limited lifestyle.

Nowadays treating phobias is considered so straightforward that cases are assigned to the psychology assistant, or even untrained helpers may administer the therapy. So what has happened between the publication of *The Locomotive God* in 1928 and today to make phobias so easy to treat? The turning point was Joseph Wolpe's book, *Psychotherapy by Reciprocal Inhibition*, published in 1958,[2] which marked the birth of behavioural therapy as a new discipline with conditioning theory as its fundamental premise. At the time, the professional climate in psychiatry and psychology was electric. Psychoanalysis had been the dominant ideology up to that point, suggesting that psychological disorder could only be helped through analysis of deep underlying causes. An upstart had come along saying there was no need for all that analysis; deconditioning was all that was required. Conferences were set up purposely pitching psychoanalysis against behaviour therapy. In one conference a rather unsuspecting R.D. Laing was set against Hans Eysenck, one of the leading proponents of behaviour therapy, who fiercely argued that psychoanalysis was unscientific, 'explaining everything and predicting nothing'. Laing's rather polite and open response was in stark contrast to Eysenck's invective. The emotional tension, fierce arguments and sense of the revolutionary new approach versus the stuffy psychoanalytic orthodoxy make conferences now seem very civilized.

Deconditioning deconstructed

Joseph Wolpe's conditioning technique called 'systematic desensitization' soon became a standard technique for treating phobic patients around the world. The conditioning idea behind this was that a phobic object (for example, an aeroplane) had accidentally become associated with the fear response. The rationale of systematic desensitization was to break down this association between the phobic object and the fear, thereby undoing the conditioned link. First, the patient was taught relaxation exercises, so as to bring muscular tension down to as low a level as possible. Relaxation was thought to be contradictory to the fear response. A 'hierarchy' of fear situations was constructed with the patient, starting with situations with just a modicum of anxiety (such as viewing aeroplanes on TV), to those with more anxiety (visiting an airport), to the top of the hierarchy (travelling on a plane). While in a state of muscular relaxation, the person imagined the least threatening situation in the hierarchy. Once they were able to relax and think of this (after about three or four occasions), they had to think of the next most difficult situation in the hierarchy while staying relaxed, all the way up to the most difficult scenario, over perhaps fifteen to twenty sessions. The principle was that a new set of conditioned associations would be set up whereby the phobic object was now associated with relaxation, not fear. Part of the rationale of the behavioural approach was that it should be open to experimental testing and a huge body of research ensued.

But the answers seemed topsy-turvy. The research indicated that the therapy was effective, but unexpected results started to be published which were eventually to turn the therapy upside down. It was found that the therapy worked as well with or without a hierarchy,[3] and that imagined situations were not as effective as those in real life,[4,5] and later investigations showed that relaxation was not necessary for successful results.[6] All the elements of the therapy that were supposed to be essential could be removed and the therapy would still be successful. What was going on?

Psychiatrist Isaac Marks at the Maudsley Hospital had spearheaded much of the research into systematic desensitization and it was he who eventually solved the puzzle. Marks[7,8] concluded that the critical ingredient in therapy was not relaxation, or hierarchies, or gradual desensitization, but what he called 'exposure in vivo'. Simply exposing the patient to the phobic stimulus for long periods of time (30–45 minutes) in real life diminished the fear sensations and helped the patient reconstruct his or her life without the domination of fear. Face the fear! Why hadn't this simple approach been discovered before? The main drawback for the behaviour therapist was that it was the *opposite* to the predictions of conditioning theory. In systematic desensitization the therapist would go to great pains to ensure that the patient never experienced an increase in tension when thinking of the phobic object. If they did they had to resume relaxing their muscles before the imagined phobic object was re-introduced. In other words the sacred belief was that therapy acted by deconditioning the association between the fear reaction and the phobic object.

Marks was able to think the impossible and state that it was simply time exposed to the fear that counted. Extreme tension can be associated with the phobic object, and it does not make an iota of difference to the outcome of therapy. Conditioning, the weapon that had successfully destroyed the dominance of psychoanalysis, had suddenly had its power removed. There were desperate attempts to recast exposure as conditioning,[9] but classical conditioning in psychological therapy was completely eclipsed. What followed was an era of really successful therapies for phobic patients based on what worked in practice – exposure in vivo – but without any real knowledge of why it was so effective. But that was not the end of it. Clinical psychologists such as Edna Foa began to show that the same principles of behavioural exposure in vivo (shortened simply to 'exposure') worked equally well in overcoming the compulsive urges that lay behind obsessional rituals and thoughts.[10] Another study demonstrated that people stuck in chronic grief could overcome this if exposed to photos, mementoes and memories of the loved one.[11] Exposure seemed to work as well with grief and compulsive urges as with anxiety and fear. The pattern of changes was so similar in these differing conditions as to suggest a universal psychological process was at work.

Behavioural exposure, just like clockwork

Now I was finding exactly the same in alcohol abuse – at first I had not conceptualized what I was doing as 'behavioural exposure' because exposure had become so associated in my mind with phobias. A colleague of mine, Richard Blakey, had tried the same approach very successfully with alcohol abuse patients, and together in 1980 we published our work under the title 'An Exposure Approach to Alcohol Abuse'.[12] Simultaneously other psychologists were experimenting with what they called 'cue exposure', which later emerged as an effective treatment for both drug and alcohol abuse.

Behavioural exposure seems to be one of the few psychotherapeutic techniques that works like clockwork. Even in quite new and surprising areas, such as excessive desire or craving, or unwanted thoughts, it seems to work equally well.

John, a young healthy-looking trainee jockey, was crippled by obsessional fears and doubts, some quite unusual. He would try to ensure he faced his colleagues at work so that he could see their lips when they spoke because otherwise he was plagued with obsessional doubts along the lines of: 'Did he really say that or was I imagining it? If I imagined it, that proves that I am losing my mind, becoming schizophrenic.' (John had experience of a close friend who had become schizophrenic so this fear always haunted him.) If he could not see their lips he would ask them again and again to repeat things to assuage his doubt, much to their irritation. Having (with great difficulty) worked out what was going on we set up a 'behavioural exposure' experiment in the therapy office. I would stand behind John (so he couldn't see my lips) and say things at different intervals and different volumes, varying my position in the room. As in Alex's case I would assess the severity of his distress on a ten-point scale. He did not shake as Alex had at the first sight of the whisky bottle, but was extremely distressed and wanted to turn to look at me or restart the experiment. His distress was sky-high, but as I spoke to him more and more behind his back his distress and doubts about what I was saying reduced to nearly nothing. If the psychologist plots these ten-point graphs over 20–25 minutes – whether it is for phobic anxiety, desire for alcohol, obsessional thoughts, doubts, or distress – the plots are as close to a straight line as you will find in psychology. There will be occasional surges in that line as the patient imagines a new fear, but by and large the graphs are pretty indicative of a biological or physiological phenomenon. It has been referred to as a sort of physiological habituation.

Behavioural exposure is so effective, so reproducible and applicable to so many behavioural problems that it stands out as one of the few hard facts in clinical psychology. But let's pause for a moment. 'Behavioural exposure' was the product of the behaviour therapy movement, but really how 'behavioural' is exposure? Although ultimately the phobic patient can do what he or she could not originally do – the obsessive patient does not carry out rituals, and the alcohol abuse patient no longer drinks alcohol – the exposure exercises focus on facing *fear*, facing *compulsive urges*, facing the *desire* to drink. Fear, urge, desire, doubt, sadness, distress – the crux of the exposure is that the distressing emotions, which initially the patient could not bear, have reduced in intensity and now become bearable, less intense, less compelling. Is this 'behavioural exposure' or is it really 'emotional exposure'? What is hidden here is a powerful, almost universal, truth about emotions. A distressing emotional feeling faced for long enough will lose its emotional power. But on the other hand, if that emotional feeling is avoided, subdued, suppressed, pushed out of sight, it remains in a time warp. It does not lose its original power – it is not dealt with, not emotionally processed. There is an effort involved in suppression, too. The feeling always has the capacity to re-emerge, always needs to be kept in its cage, needs at some subconscious level to be checked to see that it is dormant, quiet and unlikely to cause problems. Because the feeling is never faced, it is never solved.

Life's path seems to be smooth enough for long periods, but then troubles emerge in the form of accidents, illness or bereavement. Can the same exposure idea, so successful with fears and phobias, apply here too? In the next chapter I shall try to show more fully how this 'healing through feeling' principle can help with the severest trauma.

Shell Shock

The limits of endurance

'The silence woke me up. A lull in the bombardment of cannons and the whine of bullets. As soon as I was conscious, the pain hit me. After riding the first surge of agony, there came the sickening realization that I was in the middle of the battlefield and night was descending. I was terrified that at any moment an enemy scout might find me and slit my throat. Lying in the mud, my despair was heightened as I remembered awful flashes of the battle. Today was the day we had all dreaded – going over the top. Grouping in the trenches. Fixing bayonets. The whistle and "Over lads!" The crack of machine guns. Johnny had been with me since we joined up and was like a brother, like a twin. He was running beside me, then suddenly he was in pieces. Blackened pieces, unbearable noise, smoke so black, then oblivion. I must have been hit too. And here I was in the open battlefield. Could I crawl back to the trenches before first light? Would I make it? As I dragged myself along through mud, barbed wire and blackened debris, my mind was obsessed with one overwhelming fear – that I might crawl through the feet, the hands, the blood and the face of Johnny.'

In the First World War, the British Army had to deal with 80,000 cases of shell shock. Soldiers had seen friends killed or mutilated, had bayoneted 'enemy' young men much like themselves, had endured deafening bombardment by day and night, had been stuck in trenches with rats carrying syphilis, poor sanitation, cold, constantly standing in water that caused 'trench foot', with dysentery and TB raging and in fear of mustard gas attacks. Some soldiers reached the point at which they were unable to sleep, eat, had uncontrollable diarrhoea and constant crippling anxiety. Movement disorders were common, such as shaking, paralysis, facial tics, inability to walk properly, sudden jerks and tremors, and some lost the power of speech. Others experienced 'shut down' or dissociation from normal experience, in which they might wander off from the battlefield, many to be shot as deserters. Nightmares of being unable to withdraw bayonets from the enemies' bodies persisted for months after the combat. Intrusive images might occur at any time, as an infantry captain complained: 'Right in the middle of an ordinary conversation… When the face of a Bosch that I have bayoneted, with its horrible gurgle and grimace, comes sharply into view.'

Poet Vernon Scannell, who joined the army at eighteen, after five months of daily artillery and tank attacks in the Second World War desert campaign, described how he reached his limit when he saw his fellow compatriots looting the corpses of British soldiers they had been chatting with an hour before. This act of betrayal somehow marked the limit of his endurance. He turned from the battlefield and walked through the desert in a 'strange dreamlike state' that did not seem to be under his control. 'When I remember it, I seemed to be floating along rather than walking. I carried on walking and walking and covered something like 100 miles. I nearly reached Tripoli.' In the Second World War, the terms 'war neurosis' and 'battle fatigue' replaced the First World War description of 'shell shock'. The Royal Air Force did not recognize any psychological disorder, simply calling it LMF, or 'lacking in moral fibre', and discharged sufferers with no pay and having to live down the stigma of cowardice.

The effects of trauma can be seen in all military forces, of all nationalities in any war. But it is not just war that can traumatize individuals. The *Herald of Free Enterprise* Zebrugge Ferry Disaster (1987), Piper Alpha oil rig fire (1988) and Lockerbie air disaster (1988) brought to public attention how the same sort of long-term disabling anxiety that had been observed during war could also be observed in the survivors of disasters. Indeed it does not have to be a national disaster, but personal, individual disasters such as a car crash, can equally traumatize a person.

Post-traumatic stress disorder

From 1974 to 1980, leading clinicians and researchers had been drawing together information on trauma, stress and war neurosis, in preparation for the 1980 publication of the American Psychiatric Association's *Diagnostic and Statistical Manual of Mental Disorders (DSM III)*.[1] This concluded that there was a discrete, recognizable stress reaction following a traumatic event. It was labelled 'post-traumatic stress disorder' (PTSD), a diagnostic category that has stimulated much research and therapy.

The crucial trigger for developing PTSD is not war or national disaster but rather exposure to a traumatic event that threatened death or serious injury to oneself or others. The response involves intense fear, helplessness or horror. The average person walks around in a bubble of protection that assumes 'It won't happen to me.' When a traumatic event really does happen the bubble often bursts. It is the realization of imminent death that usually sets the scene for PTSD, although witnessing the death or mutilation of others is also included as a possible trigger.

The stress reaction a person experiences – so out of the ordinary – is not like the stress of exams, the dentist or public speaking. It is so different from normal experience that the person often thinks they have gone mad. There are three main groups of symptoms in the post-traumatic stress reaction.

First, there are nightmares of the traumatic event or intrusive and realistic memories during the waking hours. The experience of the infantry captain who suddenly saw the face of 'a Bosch that I have bayoneted' during an ordinary conversation is a typical example of an intrusive flashback of the trauma. Any event, word, TV programme or thought reminding the person of the trauma can trigger intense distress.

The second group of symptoms are integrally bound up with the person's style of processing difficult events. The emotional processing styles are highlighted in the *Diagnostic and Statistical Manual*. The first, more conscious, style is 'avoidance', the attempt to avoid *anything* associated with the trauma – thoughts, feelings, conversations, activities, places or people. The second is 'numbing', involving restricted ability to feel emotions, feelings of detachment, blocked-out memories of the trauma and loss of interest in important activities in life. While there is a certain amount of control in avoiding things, you cannot *do* numbing, it happens to you, a passive response.

The third group of symptoms are those of increased arousal ('hyperarousal') involving not being able to sleep, being on edge and constantly vigilant of danger, having an exaggerated startle response (the person jumps out of their skin when the phone rings), difficulty concentrating and irritability or outbursts of anger that may be totally out of character with the person. It is often this last feature that makes the person feel their personality has altered altogether.

Exposure to the memories

John Thorpe was a successful foreman – owner of a small, family-run building company that he had proudly built up over the years. He had had his share of knocks and stress in life, but had always risen above them. But a single event had turned this rather strong and successful man into someone who could hardly cope with simple everyday tasks. The solicitors dealing with his case had asked me to see him for a course of psychological therapy. The defining event for him had occurred on a pleasant sunny autumn day. His firm had rented a cement mixer and the rental company had provided an old machine where the engine was started with a cranking handle. Unfortunately the handle did not have an anti-kickback mechanism so when John started the engine the handle shot out with considerable force and hit him on the knee, propelling him back ten feet.

The severe injuries to John's knee had restricted his mobility. Before the accident, he used to walk nearly every day with his wife, enjoyed golfing, sea fishing, gardening and his greenhouse. All that stopped, so it was not surprising that he felt a sense of loss, depression and guilt about not supporting his wife. He had nightmares, flashbacks of the accident; he sweated and his heart raced whenever he thought about it. He tried desperately hard to avoid reminders of the accident, lost concentration, was irritable, had difficulty relaxing, felt angry and panicky with claustrophobic sensations. In short, he had most of the symptoms of post-traumatic stress disorder. He described it as feeling as if:

'I was in a room and there were no doors to the room. I just wanted to sleep and couldn't. The room was always encroaching… each day, it seemed closer. I had to have the (actual) doors and windows of the house open… and couldn't sleep with the lights off.'

Trauma theorists Horowitz[2] and Foa[3,4] had proposed that it is not the trauma itself that produces this traumatic stress response – only 20 per cent of people develop PTSD after a severe trauma. What of the other 80 per cent – why don't they develop trauma? The necessary condition for a natural recovery from the trauma is to 'emotionally engage'[5] with the traumatic memory, in other words to 'think about it, talk about it, allow memories of it to come to mind', thereby allowing emotional processing to proceed.[6,7]

Two emotional strategies are thought to hinder the process of recovery and make the person more susceptible to a post-traumatic stress reaction. One is the avoidance of the memory of the trauma, and the other is emotional dissociation, producing a numbing or blank effect on emotional life. Indeed, avoidance and numbing are described as *symptoms* of PTSD in the *Diagnostic and Statistical Manual*, but Horowitz and others see them as *strategies that cause* the stress reaction. Effective treatment tries to recreate what happens in natural recovery; the patient is encouraged to engage with the memory of the accident and not avoid or dissociate from it. This was the rationale for John's treatment, but this rather simple approach needs delicate handling in practice, which is why I would like to describe the treatment sessions in a bit more depth.

Although exposure to the memories of the accident is the crux of therapy, I have found that it is worthwhile spending perhaps two sessions explaining and preparing the person for therapy. They need to know in advance what will happen during therapy, and how facing the traumatic memories will ultimately diminish their hold over them; how it will be painful and difficult at first and may make them feel worse initially until the point at which the memories lose their impact. They will also need to plan how to cope with any initial disturbing reactions, informing relatives or friends and ensuring they have an understanding and supportive environment to fall back on. Some time will be spent explaining how the exposure they are about to embark on is different from brief memories they may have had, or flashbacks, or single brief descriptions given to the police or solicitor. It is all about *staying with* and even exploring the memories, not running from them; a wilful facing rather than a quick 'look and run'.

And the time spent is important too. Isaac Marks' 1970 studies on behavioural exposure explored the optimum interval of time one should spend 'exposed'. Very brief exposures could make the problem even worse, 'sensitizing' the person to the trauma. Exposures of 30–45 minutes were optimal with phobias.

It is possible that the accounts given to police or solicitors were more sensitizing than healing.

For John these discussions led him to a consideration of how he had handled thoughts of the trauma at home. He described feeling nervous when in the same room as his family in case the conversation turned to the accident. His family had learned to avoid the topic. He got so upset he found it hard to properly converse with them and spent too much energy 'fighting hard not the think of the accident'. He recounted how a former friend had been describing an accident in which he had broken his thumb. John was sweating, panicking and trying to find ways to end the conversation and get out of the room. He also recalled that even before the accident he had tried to avoid upsetting memories about childhood, and that emotional avoidance was his style for dealing with things. So in preparing for therapy like this we were not only preparing John to face memories of the trauma but also trying to reverse an ingrained style of feeling.

It was worthwhile spending time talking about emotions in general, and, as it were, preparing the soil properly. If the therapy goes against a lifelong emotional style, the person may give it lip service but not engage to the necessary level. John was very responsive to these discussions and realized his former 'closed' style of dealing with emotions was problematic. So by session three he was prepared and ready for 'the onslaught'.

The main task from session three onwards was to help John focus on the memories of the accident. He had thought about it and prepared himself for the big day. After a brief summary of the approach at the start of session three, I asked him to go back to the day of the accident and describe it in detail to me. To get things started I asked him to tell me about the day – his breakfast, going to work, the weather and so on. The details are not important in themselves but helped to transport him back to those crucial memories. It is often important to engage as many senses as possible in making the memory vivid – so the sights, sounds and smells all help to build up the total picture, and sometimes jog new memories. He described his breakfast, meeting the other men, snippets of conversation he had had with them, where the concrete mixer was standing, and was about to start describing starting the machine when I asked him to stand up and adopt the same pose as he did on that fatal day, turning the handle exactly as on the day. The use of 'proprioceptive' sense – moving, balance and muscle position – is as much part of the memory as remembering the visual scene.

As soon as he started to turn the imaginary handle in the therapist's office, his original feelings were recreated – his heart raced, he sweated and the fear flooded back. He replayed being shot backwards by the force of the handle and showed how he landed on some bags of cement stored by a wall behind him. His reaction was powerful and distressing, but he knew he had to face it. We went through the sequel: getting help from an ex-nurse, people asking him ridiculous questions, such as 'Did it hurt?', with the accompanying feelings of anger, and eventually the ambulance arriving. We went through what was said and done at the hospital, the reaction of his family that night and the progress of his pain over the next few days. By the end of the session he was exhausted yet triumphant. He had faced what he had been trying to avoid for so long. It was important, I explained, to capitalize on this and carry this on in various homework assignments. He would keep a diary of the day in as much detail as he could remember, and, importantly, he decided to talk to his wife about the accident. We arranged a further session for the next week.

In the next session, John described how memorizing the moment of the accident vividly was the turning point for him. It had been a massive reaction. John had thrown himself into the exercises with a vengeance – he had written them down at length, talked to his wife, his son, the GP.

'When I spoke to my wife I felt I had to keep talking – the whole weekend. I felt a 10-ton weight had been lifted off my shoulders. I felt emotional for the first time, more relaxed, and proud of myself. I spoke to my son for the first time.'

'How do you mean, "spoke to him for the first time"?' I queried.

'I had never spoken to him about the accident and there was a sort of tension between us – I finally talked to him about the accident for the first time.'

'Did he react badly?'

'No, he was always on tenterhooks trying not to speak about it. He'd do anything not to talk about it, because he wasn't sure how I'd take it. Not sure whether it would sort of... push me over the edge.'

'What did he say?' I ventured.

'He said it was worse than walking on eggshells. It made him feel awkward when he was with me... but now, well now – we're back together again.'

It has always seemed so strange to me that while the first event traumatized John, going through it with full emotion a second time could be so healing. You might expect it to intensify matters, but on the contrary it seemed to be a turning point in his recovery. Over the next three or four sessions we went over and over the experience again, as he remembered more and more details. Each new snippet of conversation, even the memory of a minor happening, led to new steps forward, as if he was actually happy to recall more painful memories. I suspect it was more like putting pieces of a jigsaw together, with the joy of finding that one missing piece – even though the piece depicts a scene from Hieronymus Bosch.

As we went over memories again and again, not only did they lose their power to evoke any distress or fear, but also it seemed that John had learned a new way to deal with his life. He seemed to face things head-on – and he now shared with his wife and family. There was an apparent sense of openness and sharing that had not really existed before the therapy.

The memory that got away

Jane was also referred to me by her solicitors. She had been assessed by a psychiatrist because she was still experiencing anxiety and depression one year after a minor car accident. She was not experiencing full blown post-traumatic stress disorder, with nightmares and flashbacks, but still was 'not her normal self' and found things so difficult now.

We went through the same sort of reliving the accident as with John, but with few emotions. She was able to put the accident together quite well – and although it seemed to help to discuss it, there was nothing like the breakthrough John had experienced. I was a bit bewildered so decided to go into the accident in as much detail as possible.

In my office I rearranged chairs to mock up the car in which she had had the accident while driving her baby son Ian to the babysitter. She was sitting in the 'driver's seat', imagining Ian in the back seat.

'So the other driver hit you here (indicating the front right part of the bonnet) and here (indicating rear right). Then what?'

'I stopped and just sat there.'

'What then?'

'Nothing really.'

'How did you get out of the car?'

She showed me, in the imaginary set-up we had created.

'Then what?' I asked, and it was here that the detail proved crucial.

'I couldn't go and see what had happened to Ian,' she said.

'Why not?'

There was a pause as emotion struck deep.

'I was afraid he might be all bloody and broken up.'

The tears came to her eyes with the powerful emotional realization that this was the one – the one and only – part of her memory she had suppressed. She couldn't bear to look and see him injured (which he wasn't). At once she knew that her avoidance of this one discrete memory had given her night after night of poor sleep, tension and panic. She had previously been able to recall nearly everything about the whole accident, except for this incident with Ian; she had talked about it, dealt with it, and was bewildered as to why her low-level problems persisted.

'I feel I'm back,' Jane said later. 'Back to me. I've dealt with it, put it behind me. I can move on now.'

As a postscript, in our last session she described a recent hospital visit to a friend diagnosed with cancer: 'As soon as I saw her I burst into tears and hugged her. That's not me. I usually skirt around it – "How are your feeling?" and so on – but now we can really talk about it.'

Strangely, processing emotionally one crucial memory was the doorway to Jane entering a whole new world of freer emotions.

Battened Down and Bottled Up

1,001 ways to keep it at bay

'I feel butterflies in my tummy and feel I want to cry. Then I suppress my feelings. I take a great big breath, hold it in, tense myself, or put my mind onto something else – take the dog out for a walk, do the housework. I say, 'Don't be so b– stupid; pull yourself together.'
   Rebecca M., a panic attack sufferer

'A scout smiles and whistles under all circumstances. When he gets an order, he should obey it cheerily and readily, not in a slow, hangdog sort of way. When you just miss a train, or someone treads on your corn – not that a scout ought to have such things – or under any annoying circumstances, you should force yourself to smile at once and then whistle a tune, and you will be all right.'
   Boy Scout Lore, 1908

'When Ouma Kassim (World Middleweight Boxing Champion contender) was 5¹/₂ he was kidnapped from his primary school by the rebel Ugandan National Resistance Army. Everyone in his class was taken. The first night, when he learnt the rules, haunts him particularly; if you cry, you die; if you run, you die. And a lot of boys were shot for disobeying.'
   The Times, 7 December 2006

£4,000 SNIP TO CURE BLUSHING

'British surgeons have developed a pioneering operation (endoscopic thoracic sympathicotomy) to cure blushing. Using keyhole surgery… a nerve of the sympathetic nervous system is cut. "The mechanism is that the regulation of the blood vessels of the skin is controlled by this nerve. It dilates the small blood vessels of the skin. The nerve cannot be controlled by your own will, it is an automatic function," said Christer Drott, a vascular surgeon at Highgate Hospital in London… "The nerve is also an accelerator for the heart, and the heart rate is reduced… The cutting of the nerve also affects sweating, increasing it below the chest and lowering it above."'

   Daily Telegraph, 14 May 2000

'The growing practice of providing professional counselling for anyone who has a stressful experience was questioned by the Princess Royal yesterday. In a blunt address to a Victim Support conference in Glasgow, she said that most people were sufficiently intelligent to cope with stress without professional help. She suggested that Post-Traumatic Stress Disorder might be no more than a convenient label for a common problem. The Princess, who was the target of a failed kidnap attempt in The Mall in 1974, said that victims were stronger than they were given credit for.'

   Daily Telegraph, 24 February 1996

'The way I cry is with earphones and put Tchaikovsky or Beethoven's 6th on with a glass of Scotch and cry over the interpretation of the music, not because I feel sad.'

   J.T., former Sergeant Major

These quotes, taken from very varied sources, highlight some common reactions to the issue of dealing with emotional experiences. The list of ways in which individuals try to suppress emotion is extensive and includes:

- distraction
- avoiding reminders
- alcohol
- illegal drugs
- food
- endoscopic thoracic sympathicotomy
- antidepressants
- anxiety-reducing drugs
- sleeping tablets
- self-hypnosis
- cutting oneself
- dissociation
- positive thinking
- keeping an even keel
- memory loss
- suppressing thoughts
- anaesthetizing one's feelings
- switching to another personality
- pretending it didn't happen
- keeping busy
- never stopping or relaxing

Some of these mechanisms may be quite benign and even positive. An ice skater performing for a competition cannot afford to let regret or self-recrimination interfere with her performance after slipping over. It's 'up and concentrate on the rest of the act', remaining positive in order to salvage the performance. Allowing emotions to be fully felt would probably mean losing the competition. This type of suppression is unlikely to do her any emotional harm at all. Other types of suppression may be far more harmful, and corrosive, such as refusing to cry or show 'weakness' at the death of a close family member. Often it is not just a single 'act of suppression' but more a style of dealing with emotions that may have developed from childhood upwards and typically repeats again and again over the years.

Not here and not now

So why do people suppress emotions? In the main, the answer is quite simple. Emotions, or to be specific, negative emotions, are painful to experience. The more severe the experience, such as mugging or rape, the harder the emotion is to bear. Thinking about the event recreates many of the original unbearable feelings and sensations, and who wants that? Also, it is not just facing the emotions, but also the memory of the situation that originally evoked it. The emotions and the situation are integrally fused, so that it is rather like reliving the trauma or the hurt again. Therefore, why not use the 1,001 devices at our disposal to sidestep, avoid, suppress or distract from the emotional pain? The logic is obvious: Who wants their hand burnt? – take it off the stove. Who wants emotional pain? – remove the thoughts and memories.

Suppression is not always a strategy for avoiding facing painful memories; the woman whose husband dies may not cry at the funeral, not so much as to avoid facing the pain but to avoid upsetting or embarrassing her children. For many men crying was once seen as weakness – not so much in today's Britain – but negative attitudes to emotions can also shape what we show and do not show to others. Marjorie (see Chapter 1) could not cry, not because she disliked difficult emotional experience, but through her harsh childhood training 'not to blab like a baby'.

But often, emotional pain is just hard to bear. And suppression, in its many guises, is the device to save us from further pain.

The problem is, suppression does not work very well. It may work in the short term – it means we do not have to feel the emotional pain *now*. But significant emotional pain does not go away of its own accord. Time doesn't heal. The pain remains buried. It is stored in ice, like an ice-age corpse preserved over the ages and discovered almost intact centuries later. If the event was simply tucked away, not considered, not thought about, not discussed, not worked out, not expressed – in other words, not properly processed emotionally – it has the capacity to affect us when we are not prepared. An accidental reminder, a scene or a phrase on TV, a newspaper article, a chance remark in a conversation, could trigger the memory. Occasionally it can trigger a disconnected version of the trauma, in which the power of the suppressed emotion is felt without the awareness of the context or meaning, which can be frightening and perplexing. The more appalling the memory, such as sexual abuse in childhood, the harder it is to access. The person may have forgotten the experience, automatically cut themselves off from it; but reminders of it can still cause a sense of unease. It is possible in therapy to retrieve lost memories by purposely remembering dates, family occasions, the layout of a room, what pop songs were playing at the time and many other memory joggers.

Psychotherapists have noted how vivid, detailed and powerful traumatic memories can be. While there is much criticism over the validity of past memories in court cases, the American psychologist Gordon Allport argued in the 1950s that:

> '… it is unlikely (barring repression) that individuals will forget the emotional, ego-charged personality-forming experiences of their lives. Inaccurate as testimony often is in respect to detail, the memory for salient facts, for atmosphere, and for experiences most closely related to the self is trustworthy.'[1]

Experiencing the pain

The central part of 'healing through feeling' is allowing oneself to re-experience the emotional pain – not just for a millisecond or at arm's length – but to really engage with it and feel it. Zoe, a patient whom I was treating for post-traumatic stress reactions following a car crash in which her husband was badly injured, explained that there seemed to be three levels of 'feeling'. One was replaying the memory of the car crash in a rather objective way, just remembering events but keeping emotion at arm's length. The second level Zoe described was remembering the car crash while feeling emotional. The third, or ultimate, level, was a vivid reliving of the crash, almost as if it was happening, in which the sights, the smells, the sounds, the bodily sensations and the entire emotional context, were fully present. She was describing this in the context of homework assignments I had given her, asking her to remember and write down her memory of the car crash in detail. In the privacy of her own home she could no doubt control the level at which she remembered the crash. But in the therapy office, when she was asked to describe the experience in detail, it was less easy to keep such control. One memory can lead to another and suddenly the emotions are evoked in full power.

While it is not absolutely necessary to experience the 'full power of emotions' for therapy to be effective, it is important to connect with emotions at least at some level. The purpose of facing the feelings is to allow the natural sequence of emotional processing to occur. The person feels and acknowledges the central pain face on; they grapple with it; stay with it long enough for it to lose its terrifying impact. They also stay with it long enough to start to consider solutions: talking about it; seeing things differently; changing their life; confronting the perpetrator; crying, grieving, shouting; taking action; hitting out. This sort of processing can never occur if the memory is locked in a cupboard, kept in the past, put into deep freeze.

Suppression, avoidance and dissociation are temporary solutions to avoid feeling the pain *now*, but they do not allow emotional processing to start. Allowing oneself to feel and face the emotional memories is the first step towards releasing the natural power of emotional processing. Facing emotional memories ultimately robs the memory of its emotional power. Suppression ensures that the emotional power is locked in the body.

Can emotions be bottled up?

But how does the body retain the emotional power of the memories year after year, and how can it relinquish that power so easily? In English, if we talk about 'bottling up our emotions', it is easily understood; we all know what bottling up means. This only became clear to me when Professor Paola Gremigni and Mariaelisa Santonastaso, Italian research psychologists working with our research team, translated the Emotional Processing Scale into Italian. One of the phrases was 'I bottled up my emotions'. This was changed to '*Ho bloccato le mie emozioni*' ('I blocked my emotions') in translation. However, we noticed that the same translation was also used for the phrase 'I switched off my emotions'. It was only after careful discussion that we discovered that this metaphor of bottling emotions, as if we would bottle up champagne, was not widely used in Italy. The idea seems quite important for the British. It conveys the notion that strong feelings are contained, or bottled, and the pressure, like bubbly champagne, is contained within and capable of bursting the cork and bubbling out if given half the chance.

A number of types of psychotherapeutic methods are based on the idea of 'releasing' this pressure or tension. As mentioned in Chapter 1, the hydraulic metaphor is often ascribed to Freud. It refers to a sort of system of water pipes; pressure can build up in one part of the system and can cause an overflow elsewhere if suddenly released. Perhaps the most famous of 'hydraulic' therapies is Janov's 'primal scream' therapy, involving, as the name suggests, howling, screaming and bodily expressing deep underlying tensions so that they are released and freedom is found. John Lennon was personally treated by Janov using primal scream therapy in the 1960s when it was at the apex of its popularity. A review of cathartic therapies suggests that they rely on the idea of 'bottling up' in quite a literal sense; that negative energy or power is stored in the body, which is harmful to the individual and needs to be released. This has been called a 'container model' – that emotions can be stored as if in a container somewhere in the body. Surveys carried out on large groups in the UK or US suggest that many people subscribe to the idea that it is unhealthy to 'store up' emotions and that they need to be released. But the simple idea that the emotions can be stored has its strong critics. Where are they stored and how? How can they be kept in a mental container for many years? What about when you sleep and totally relax, how can this tension still be retained?

Although this idea of pressure, energy, power, hydraulics, the storing up of emotional pressure is ascribed to Freud, he is quite clear thinking about this and actually puts forward a different explanation. In the following passage from Freud's *Selected Papers on Hysteria*[2] he offers an explanation of how powerful unresolved emotions can exert their influence over an individual:

'It would seem at first rather strange that long-forgotten experiences should exert so intensive an influence and that their recollections should not be subject to the decay into which all our memories sink. We will perhaps gain some understanding of these facts by the following examinations.

The blurring or loss of an affect [felt emotional aspect] of memory depends on a great many factors. In the first place, it is of great consequence whether there was an energetic reaction to the affectful experience. By reaction we here understand a whole series of voluntary or involuntary reflexes ranging from crying to an act of revenge through which, according to experience, affects are discharged. If the success of this reaction is of sufficient strength, it results in the disappearance of a great part of the affect. Language attests to this fact of daily observation in such expressions as "to give vent to one's feelings", to be "relieved by weeping" etc. If the reaction is suppressed, the affect remains united with the memory. An insult retaliated, be it only in words, is differently recalled than one that had to be taken in silence... the reaction of an injured person to a trauma has really only then a perfect "cathartic" effect if it is expressed in an adequate reaction like revenge. But more likely man finds a substitute for this action in speech through which help the affect can well-nigh be ab-reacted.'

Clearly, Freud did not see emotions as being stored, kept contained, within the mind. Memory is the key. What is problematic is the stored affect-laden memory. Lutz, in his excellent text on tears, summarizes the issue rather well:

'The emotions we feel as we relive past experiences are simply a coming to consciousness of one's desires. We cannot feel the same emotions because they are long gone. Emotions cannot be stored for years in our bodies, waiting to reappear, like a virus or bottled up carbonation. We might cry, of course, in a way very similar to the way we cried when our desires were first frustrated, but not because the tears have been waiting somewhere inside us during the intervening years. We cry because the events or the desires still invoke powerful feelings when they are remembered or recognized, in part because our understanding of the events has not evolved.'[3]

There is here a parallel between psychotherapy and everyday life. In psychotherapy there are often traumatic or disturbing events that have not been dealt with, and the therapist acts to steer the process of emotional recovery. The majority of life's stresses, strains and hurts, 'slings and arrows of outrageous fortune', are dealt with in everyday life without the assistance of a therapist, but the process of recovery in psychotherapy and everyday life may be remarkably similar. In both instances, difficult emotional events need to be emotionally processed in such a way that they no longer trouble us, do not absorb any more time and mental energy in trying to suppress or endlessly ruminating, and are no longer an aggravation to our physiological bodily system.

Three elements in emotional processing

It would seem that there are three major stages or psychological mechanisms underpinning the emotional recovery, the emotional processing of hurt and trauma:

1. **Facing** This involves recalling and living with difficult memories of the event, re-experiencing emotions evoked by that memory without trying to suppress, avoid or cut oneself off from the emotional pain. The psychological process at work involves exposure to the physiological sensations, arousal and memories, to everything that constitutes the emotional situation. As Isaac Marks' research showed, the exposure needs to be sustained over a good period of time.

2. **Catharsis** The release of emotional feelings, the reliving and pouring out of what happened and all that the experience meant to us. Crying is like a microcosm of full-blown catharsis. In the final scene of *Marnie*, Hitchcock's wonderfully psychoanalytical thriller about a disturbed woman, Marnie relives the night as a child in which she killed a sailor who was attempting to have sex with her mother. The repressed memory had blighted Marnie's life and led to a range of perplexing psychological symptoms. This reliving was so evocative that Marnie even reverted to her childlike voice. Despite its Hollywood take, this is a classic example of catharsis. For most people trauma and emotional hurts are not on this dimension, not necessarily beyond consciousness, as Marnie's was. At the less severe end of the spectrum this could be referred to as 'emotional

release' or 'emotional expression', for instance, a woman tearfully explaining to her lover how rejected she felt by his behaviour.

Catharsis involves many different therapeutic elements. It may include confession, disclosure of secrets or things kept hidden, revealing oneself to another, the shame of our actions listened to and accepted by another person, unconditional acceptance of me-as-a-person and the expression of pent-up feelings.

3. **Understanding the situation** This stage may also be referred to as 're-framing', 're-conceptualizing', 'working through', 'working out issues', or 'making closure'. With my patients I usually describe this as 'putting the pieces of the jigsaw together.

It is impossible to solve or work out the repercussions of a difficult life event until it is first recalled, faced and accepted. All the myriad details need to be 'worked through', which entails thinking about the events long enough to spark off the other memories, or trains of thought, that accompanied the event. Every 'piece of the jigsaw' needs to be put into place. Many everyday crises may be like a child's jigsaw with only five pieces, but significant traumas often carry a complex jigsaw of thoughts, feelings, actions, perceptions, decisions and repercussions. Understanding all the different aspects can only be achieved when the jigsaw is complete.

These three steps – facing, expressing and understanding – may occur in a small way every day as part of the normal emotional processing of the stresses and hassles of daily life, but are particularly important in the therapy of serious life traumas and hurts.

PART IV

How to Sabotage Healing

Love and Pasta

The emotion rulebook

The mountain pathway that runs down from the mountain village of San Rocco, overlooking the Golfo Paradiso in northern Italy, winds past smallholdings, orchards, gardens and vineyards perched, terraced style, on the mountainside, until it reaches the seaside town of Camogli. On a warm September evening, around dusk, as I walked down the path, I could hear a family having its evening meal in the garden. The wall beside the path and the overhanging vines did not allow me to get much of a glimpse, but it sounded as if there was a mother and father with their children, someone from an older generation, possibly a grandmother or grandfather, and some other relatives or friends. I thought at first that father had lost his temper and was shouting at everybody, but no one seemed in the least concerned and they all shouted back with equal gusto. Actually the conversations were not sequential and orderly but spoken over each other, with explosive disagreements, counter-arguments and complaints poured into a general 'soup' of conversation while father doggedly continued to make his point. What the point was, I do not know, because I cannot speak Italian, but everyone seemed quite happy with what sounded to me like a tiny slice of chaos.

When I was at school I was baffled by the existence of a subject called English Language. English Literature, the beauties of Shakespeare, Milton and D.H. Lawrence, I could understand, but why do you need a subject teaching you about rules that you have learned and unconsciously understood since you first began to speak? I passed the exam but never quite came to grips with the idea. In the same way that people know the implicit rules of grammar that guide their speech, so they also absorb, quite unconsciously, quite naturally, implicit rules about emotion; what emotions are acceptable; to what degree they are allowed to, or should, experience each type of emotion; how positive and negative emotions should be expressed, or, in the case of Britain – land of the stiff upper lip – should not be expressed. These rules are never spelt out, never official, never brought to the surface, never written down, yet they exert a covert and unconscious guidance on how individuals should feel, how they should be, and how they should express themselves. For our Italian family even the children have absorbed the idea that animated speech and arguments are normal and acceptable, that it is OK to be excitable, and that their feelings should be expressed openly. For other families a reverse set of rules might apply – that arguments are a sign that something is very wrong indeed and should not be allowed to happen.

This last section of the book may appear a little negative. The idea is to explore some of the factors that can *impede* emotional healing. In this 'Love and Pasta' chapter I shall examine the whole issue of an emotional 'rulebook' and the way negative 'rulebooks' blight the capacity to tune in accurately to one's emotions and those of others. In Chapter 11, 'A Pill for the Body, Soul and Spirit' the issue of a somatic focus to life is considered, where the whole meaning of an emotion can be missed, resulting in the quest for another pill, potion or alternative therapy to cure what is essentially an emotional problem. In Chapter 12, 'Ruminating Your Life Away', the effect of not being able to get an emotional situation out of the mind is examined. There seems to be a demarcation between normal rumination and chronic rumination. The chronic version can become so entrenched as to impair the ability for 'healing through feeling'. These chapters describe three negative emotional habits that can put emotional processing 'on hold', making that longed-for healing so elusive.

Cultural rulebooks, or simply genetic?

At a conference recently where I was describing emotional processing to a mainly medical audience, a consultant diabetician colleague asked me how much of emotional processing was genetic. I dismissed genetics as having no role at all, but afterwards realized I had been rather too hasty in my reply and started to reconsider whether genetics played any role in the expression of our emotions. In *The Expression of the Emotions in Man and Animals*,[1] Charles Darwin was the first writer to address what drives our emotional expression. He proposed that emotions have biologically fixed modes of expression that can be found in all cultures with similarities right across the animal kingdom. The book failed to have much impact on nineteenth-century thinking and nearly disappeared from sight until resurrected by evolutionary psychologists such as Paul Ekman and Carol Izard in the 1970s and 1980s. The idea is that there is a biologically fixed number of 'basic emotions' that not only have the same meaning across all cultures of the world, but have the same feelings associated with them, the same physiological patterns of reaction, the same distinctive facial expressions, distinctive changes in voice and similar ways of thinking about the emotional stimulus. The six universal emotions proposed by Ekman and his colleagues Friesen and Ellsworth in 1982 are 'anger, disgust, fear, joy, sadness and surprise'.[2]

In 1990 psychologists Ortony and Turner, in an article called 'What's Basic About Basic Emotions?',[3] conducted a review of different theories of what constitute the 'basic emotions'. From fourteen different theories, the problem is that no two lists of 'universal emotions' are the same. The different theories propose that there might be any number of basic emotions from 2 to a maximum of 11. In addition, 8 of the theories describe a 'basic emotion' that is *not* mentioned by any of the other 13 theories, including acceptance, courage, hope, contempt and guilt.

However, such theories are not always received with acclaim, as linguist Anna Wierzbicka explains:

'I experience a certain unease when reading claims of this kind... If lists such as the one above are supposed to enumerate universal human emotions, how is it that these emotions are all so neatly identified by means of English words? For example, Polish does not have a word corresponding exactly to the English word 'disgust'. What if the psychologists working on the 'fundamental human emotions' happened to be native speakers of Polish rather than English? And Australian Aboriginal language Gidjingali does not seem to distinguish lexically 'fear' from 'shame', subsuming feelings kindred to those identified by the English words for 'fear' and 'shame' under one lexical item (Hiatt, 1978). If the researchers happened to be native speakers of Gidjingali rather than English, would it still have occurred to them to claim that fear and shame are both fundamental human emotions, discrete and clearly separated from each other?'[4]

She goes on to illustrate the problem posed by different languages by exploring the meaning of the Polish word *tęsknota* (noun) / *tęsknić* (verb). She explains that if a teenage daughter leaves the family home and goes to study in a distant city, her Polish parents would usually *tęsknić.* One could not say they felt 'homesick' for their daughter, and 'nostalgia' or 'pining' do not fit. Saying they 'missed' her implies so much less than *tęsknić.* The nearest one could come would be 'pain of distance'. It would appear that this has its roots in Polish history, when, after the defeat of the Polish Uprising in 1830,

111

the 'Great Emigration' meant that the most influential Polish literature amongst the émigrés was dominated by the theme of nostalgia. The new meaning of the word *tęsknota* reflected a predominant national pre-occupation with nostalgia, not paralleled in British history.

Philosophers and existential psychologists also have a problem with the idea of fixed biological blocks of emotions, because the context in which the emotion occurs, and its subtle change over time, may be paramount, such as the evolving jealousy and possessiveness of a person as their partner becomes more distant. While biological aspects to emotion must necessarily be involved when one has a biological body, universal emotions would not appear to capture the complexity of human emotions.

Returning to the Italian family having its evening meal in the garden in San Rocco, it is likely that their children's biological capacity to feel emotions such as anger will be similar to a British child, but the rules surrounding how and when they should be noticed, experienced and expressed will differ markedly. There is an ongoing debate between the genetic and cultural perspectives that is by no means over yet.[5]

Culture is only one aspect, though. There are huge variations in how individual families within a culture experience and express emotions. It would be hard to find two families with exactly the same set of rules for emotions, and in addition different members of the same family will have different rules owing to their position in the family, their personal experiences, their gender, appearance, temperament, and so on. Also, emotional processing is not so much about the raw emotions felt (anger, frustration, anxiety, etc.), but how the emotion is processed – how it is registered, understood and expressed – and the meanings attached to it. The mechanisms a person uses for processing anger may be different from those for fear, although there could be big overlaps. For instance, someone may find any negative emotion intolerable and may try to avoid any feelings that begin to stir.

I was very surprised in a recent emotional processing therapy course, when I asked participants to identify a positive emotion they had experienced in the previous week. Later, in an experiential exercise called the 'red carpet', they had to stand on the carpet at the place that indicated how much they accepted or welcomed the emotion. Standing on the right side of the carpet represented acceptance of an emotion and standing on the left represented being ill at ease with it. For emotions such as anger or sadness it was not surprising that many participants stood towards the left of the carpet, indicating rejection of the emotion. But the surprising finding was that many people were similar when it came to positive emotions they had identified. They stood on the left or near the middle of the carpet. I had wrongly assumed that everybody wanted to experience positive emotions. Some people saw even positive emotions as disturbing and uncomfortable.

So is emotional processing style genetically determined before birth? If you or I were switched at birth and accidentally despatched to the family in San Rocco for our entire childhood, would our emotional processing style be just as it is today?

'Terry's armour'

When I first met Terry, he looked as if there was a pressure inside him. As he described his pent-up feelings, his physical features and demeanour expressed a sense of emotions closely held in check. His face and cheeks were flushed, he looked uncomfortable and hounded, his shoulders were tense and he was generally on edge. I worried about his blood pressure when I saw him go so red.

Terry's main fear was of 'losing it'. What he meant by this was losing his temper, losing his tightly held self-control and hitting someone who had been purposely goading him. Unfortunately this was a daily challenge because someone or other seemed always to be purposely goading him. His life appeared to be full of idiots whose main intention seemed to be to aggravate him. He constantly had to keep himself in check. What a strain! If he felt emotions stirring, particularly angry emotions, this was a special danger point that required vigilance and control. Terry was in a constantly wound-up state, like a coiled spring. Despite his attempts to control himself he was often abusive and rude to those he thought had offended him and occasionally he hit them. He had separated from his wife, whom he loved, many years before and was estranged from his two daughters, through his suspicious and difficult behaviour.

Yet Terry was a pleasant, kind-hearted man who wanted to get his family back and live peaceably with others. He was trying hard with this uncharted psychological therapy territory. Throughout therapy, Terry had the greatest difficulty accepting that it was his perception of others that was the problem, and that the world was not populated by idiots waiting to aggravate him. Despite many attempts, he was unable to cry or let go of the mass of deep emotional hurt that was imprisoned within. If anyone was a picture of unprocessed emotional hurts it was Terry.

Quite late on in therapy he started to talk about anger and reveal the sad story. During his childhood he had been regularly goaded, criticized and shouted at by his father.

'Did he beat you up at all?' I asked, to be greeted with an incredulous smile, as if I was an idiot.

'Regularly?' I volunteered gingerly.

'Every day.' He had been beaten with a belt, canes, sticks, by being punched and having things thrown at him. His mother, too, was beaten, and if he tried to intervene to save her, he was thrashed. Retaliation was useless, that was, until he was an adolescent. One day the table turned and he beat his father severely. That was the last occasion he was attacked, and his father disappeared from the scene soon afterwards. But the psychological repercussions lasted a lifetime.

When I asked about tears, Terry said that he had not cried since this final confrontation with his father. He said, 'I don't

cry – it's a way of getting back at him. I've never cried since.'
Crying seemed like showing weakness, and if he did cry it
seemed to him that his father would have won. This
impenetrable armour protected Terry from the world, but his
hurt was also imprisoned within that armour.

After this revelation, it was easier to understand why he
perceived others (usually men) as against him, or, to put it
another way, why he had developed a negative emotion schema
around the theme of others goading him.

Emotion schemas

'Emotion schemas' refer to the way in which these implicit
emotional rules are organized, laid down in memory during our
childhood, and influence a person's life and behaviour for
many years, sometimes for a lifetime. They refer to the way
people feel about themselves and which emotions come most
easily to them. They also refer to how individuals relate to
others; how they read other people's emotions and reactions,
how they expect them to react, and how they should express
their feelings. They are part of the personality. Emotion
schemas, which develop early in life, can be incredibly
enduring. One study found that bad temperedness in early
childhood predicted an angry orientation to life in adults
assessed thirty years later.[6] In a review of aggressive reaction
patterns in males, another study claimed that the stability of
aggressiveness was almost as high as the stability of IQ scores
over time.[7] The same has been found with shyness[8] and
sadness.[9]

Mostly emotion schemas are positive and healthy – that the
world is OK; other people like me; others can be trusted; I am
able to love others and they are able to love me. But sometimes
an emotion schema can be self-destructive, such as 'whatever I
do is not quite good enough'. The psychologists Jeffrey Young
and Janet Klosko, who worked closely with Aaron Beck, the
founder of cognitive therapy, describe eleven different types of

schema, which they refer to as 'life-traps'. These range from 'I'll never get the love I need' (emotional deprivation) and 'I can't make it on my own' (dependence) to 'I can have whatever I want' (entitlement) and 'I don't fit in' (social exclusion).[10]

But self-help is not easy. People do not usually realize that they have an emotion schema. Schemas are automatic and usually regarded as reality rather than a way of viewing the world. 'This is what it is like for me and for the rest of humanity too. An objective reality.'

If schemas were laid down after we had developed our verbal capacity as a set of verbal, logical rules, things would not be so bad. We could more easily 'talk sense to our self'. As described in the first part of this book, 'The Secret Life of the Emotions', Wilma Bucci suggests that 'the emotion schemas begin to develop in non-verbal form, including sub-symbolic images from the beginning of life; later, linguistic components are incorporated as well'.[11] What she calls 'sub-symbolic images' refers to the storing of memories relating to bodily sensations of heat, noise, sights and sounds of internal (visceral) sensations, such as pain and discomfort, and motor sensations (feelings of one's own movement). These are all automatically and unconsciously laid down before a single word is understood and spoken. They operate with a different set of processing rules than words. Our total experience as an adult combines all these different non-verbal and verbal elements, but it is the 'sub-symbolic' elements that dominate emotion schemas. And these are the elements not easily reached by verbal reasoning.

Psychologists Jennifer Jenkins and Keith Oatley, in discussing the development of emotion schemas in children, explain that the prevailing emotions expressed in the home are often built into a schema of expectation about life.[12] One-off events are less significant than repeated expressions of a similar emotional experience (good or bad). Events of a central significance to the person become an organizing structure for subsequent experience. The emotion becomes a central feature of what they expect to feel when with other people – those feelings that rise up most easily – and how they will react; in short, that which to them is normal and real. An emotion schema also acts like a self-fulfilling prophecy. Because the person is primed to perceive, for instance, a sense of failure in life, they will notice failure more often, which serves as 'proof' to confirm that this perception was correct.

Listen to your emotions... but

In Chapter 4, I explained that individuals had a sort of 'sixth sense', something like an emotional version of 'extrasensory perception'. By listening to emotional feelings people had the means to understand others more accurately and also to be aware of important issues in their own lives. But there is one important proviso to this. It is that they do not have a pervasive negative emotional schema. If, for instance, someone believed that they were worthless, and contact with others continually appeared to confirm this deficiency, such an emotional schema would seriously blight any natural ability to correctly tune in to other people. The person would spend so much energy grieving their defects that there would be little space to understand others or themselves. This is an extreme example, but listening to emotions requires at least understanding and taking account of personal emotional biases and vulnerabilities. It is this understanding that makes it more likely that a person can correctly read what their body is saying and be open to the emotions of others. I suppose this is what is meant by the old adage 'Know Thyself'.

Schemas and emotional processing

The implication for emotional processing is that negative schemas lead people to interpret too many situations as upsetting. Coming back to our original diagram of emotional processing, Figure 5 (see page 118) shows the place of past memories and schemas in the model of emotions. The emotion experienced depends on the way an event is interpreted or appraised. However, the person's emotion schemas influence the appraisal. Ideally the schemas are realistic, but a schema based around negative childhood experiences can distort the current perception of 'reality'.

Figure 5: The role of schemas

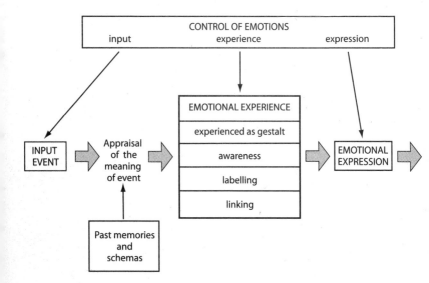

In other words, a predominantly negative schema, whether it be angry, like Terry's, or self-deprecating ('I've done it again, I'm so useless'), or socially anxious ('I'm always making a fool of myself'), will lead the person to wrongly appraise things that others do or say. In describing Terry, I have painted rather an extreme picture of someone with a fixated viewpoint. It is more likely that most people have mild tendencies to view events in certain ways, and they may well be open to reconsidering their perceptual bias. Despite prolonged individual and group psychotherapy, Terry, unfortunately, still sees the world as against him. In emotional processing terms, a negative schema will generate huge amounts of unnecessary distress for the person, which in turn needs to be emotionally processed. In effect, a negative schema will send emotional processing into overdrive.

A Pill for the Body, Soul and Spirit

Deception

'I was so happy and content. I had always wanted a child and I dreamt about how Malcolm would be a proud father and me an adoring mother; the joy a new baby would bring; how it would draw us closer together. It was like a bright new world opening up before me. And Malcolm was more loving than ever before. He brought me flowers, cosseted me and told me I was the girl for him. I wanted to please him so much.

'One day when he was away on one of his extended business trips I thought it would be a nice gesture if I had some of his business suits cleaned, went to his wardrobe and laid three of his suits on the bed. I took the hangers off and started to check if there were any coins or anything like that in the pockets before they went off to the cleaners. Well, there was something in this pocket – a piece of paper that had been folded over and over again into a compact square. I opened it fold after fold and saw it was a receipt: "Regency Jewellers, Carlisle. One ruby and diamond necklace. £950.00."

'That was a huge amount in the 1960s. I couldn't work it out. Was it a present to celebrate my pregnancy? It couldn't be – it was dated November, two months earlier. And anyway Malcolm had always said jewellery was overrated and that I needed nothing else *with a natural beauty like mine. Aside from my wedding ring he had never bought me jewellery – it made no sense.*

'I was in turmoil. I knew when I married him he would always be a bit of a Jack the Lad; he had made a pass at Tilly, my best friend, but he said it was only a bit of fun and that we were all drunk at the time. But an expensive necklace like this!

'When he returned I showed him the receipt and said, "What do you make of this?" He ranted and raved about me going through his private things just like a private detective. When he calmed down I insisted he explain it to me. Eventually he confessed that there had been a girl in Carlisle, but they had had a big bust up and it was over now. He said it had made him realize how much he loved me and I was the only girl for him. I think that was the start of it all…

'I thought it was a one-off situation, but it was only the beginning.'

This was not what I had planned for my first psychological interview with Christine McKenzie. The story of infidelity bore no resemblance to the problem described by her GP in his letter of referral to me. She had been treated over the previous four years by Dr Fraser Lamont, Consultant Rheumatologist at the Royal Aberdeen Infirmary. She had been diagnosed with fibromyalgia – constant pain in multiple areas of her body, for which no organic cause had been found – chronic fatigue and for 'query' osteoarthritis, for which she had been given injections in her hip. The GP went on:

'Over the last six months or so she has felt a deterioration in her memory and concentration. She has been on Fluoxetine [an antidepressant] for many years and in October of last year we tried increasing the dose from 20 mg to 40 mg; however, this brought no improvement in her symptoms. She discussed her symptoms with Dr Lamont at her appointment in December of last year, when he reported "she certainly

describes classical features of cognitive impairment that we see in people with chronic pain". Mrs McKenzie would be grateful for your expert opinion regarding her cognitive functioning and any advice you can give regarding her future management.'

Psychometric tests

So there I was, ready for an assessment interview in which I would administer various psychological psychometric assessments and try to pinpoint any specific cognitive difficulties. I had even obtained a copy of the *Everyday Memory Questionnaire*, which assesses whether memory lapses are within the normal range compared with a person's age group.

She started the interview by describing her medicines in great detail. As well as the Fluoxetine, she was taking Zomorph, a slow-release painkiller, Co-codamol for pain, Valsartan for hypertension, Bendrofluazide, a diuretic, Hypromellose eye drops for dry eyes, Alendronic Acid for post-menopausal symptoms, Lansoprazole for stomach problems, and Zopiclon to help her sleep. It was quite difficult to establish a rapport and to explain to her that the purpose of the interview was partly to understand her problem and partly to complete psychometric assessments, but eventually I was able to break in, asking her to explain what sort of help she wanted. She said she had noticed how her pain was everywhere, like toothache, in her hands, shoulders and legs, but not always in the same place. She had been seeing Dr Lamont for this, but in the last six months she had noticed her concentration had deteriorated. She could not even read a newspaper and had to give up her computer course at college. Her memory was appalling too – she could not remember names, dates or appointments, and would find herself in a room in her house and forget why she had gone there. She generally felt anxious and upset and was not sleeping properly. Dr Lamont had told her that memory problems were often part of chronic pain and had recommended that she come to see me for help. She was worried that fibromyalgia (which many rheumatologists regard as a medical label for chronic pain) was 'spreading' and might be causing brain deterioration. She was afraid it might be the start of dementia and hoped I could check it out and tell her how serious and advanced it was.

It was then that I asked Christine that fatal question, which caused the interview to swerve off in a totally new direction: 'What had happened in the few months before the start of your concentration problem?' This was a crucial question because it tried to identify an obvious source of psychological stress that might have set off the problem. (The person may never previously have seen the link between their physical problem and a psychological trigger.)

She explained that her husband had died nine months before and that she had had to take early retirement three months later through incapacity. In asking about her husband and the retirement, she again brought the topic back to her memory loss, poor concentration and whether it was early dementia. Three times her answer to questions about her husband was to talk about the memory loss symptoms, and on the last time she bluntly said, 'But what has this got to do with assessing my memory?'

I was almost tempted to begin the *Everyday Memory Questionnaire* then and there, but held off, feeling that there was something else that was important. At first she gave me only brief descriptions about her husband but then referred to 'an affair for twelve years'.

'An affair?' I innocently asked.

'Yes, he went off with a Thai woman.' It was as if a dam had burst. Once she had told me about this, the painful story of her husband's repeated adulterous affairs began to pour out. And as it did, the extent of his betrayal became more and more apparent, and the unfolding narrative was almost too unbearable to hear. By the end of the session she had completely abandoned her focus on her physical 'symptoms' and was instead telling me the untold story of her psychological pain. Her words at the end of our first session quite astutely summarized the issue. She said, 'I think I had switched off the painful memories.'

From soma to psyche

As Christine McKenzie's sessions continued, her painful joints, memory problems and poor concentration were never mentioned, unless I specifically asked, and I never did get to do any psychometric tests. She needed to express a lifetime of betrayal and hurt that ran deep, with many unexplained blanks owing to her husband's complex pattern of deception. It took another nine sessions for the full story to emerge. Christine had dearly loved her husband, despite repeated adulterous affairs. After a few sessions she realized, 'I was living in a fool's paradise.' Although she knew about the affairs, she always excused him or accepted his version of events. Her love for him was such that she partly denied the facts and lived in this twilight world in which hope was kept alive. 'I used to pray every night that we would grow old together. I prayed for it to be nice because I suspected things.' In the last few years before his death he told her he had married a Thai woman and started a family in Thailand. For the most part, he then disappeared from her life but inexplicably would regularly phone her from abroad and lived with her when he was in England. She could not understand this.

Emotionally, the event that brought her physical pain, fatigue and memory problems to a head was his death. (Many more details about his deception emerged as her solicitor tied up his affairs.) She both loved her husband still and was extremely angry with him for abandoning her. 'I had to cement over the problems, so I couldn't grieve for him,' she confessed. As she opened up during our sessions she was able to express her sense of anger, abandonment and grief as well as explore exactly what had been going on, trying to make sense of her emotional pain. In short, she started the work of emotional processing. This had not been possible while she was so fixed on her physical problems, which were like a boulder blocking the entrance to the real source of pain. Emotional processing could only begin once she accepted the validity of her emotional hurt.

As she described him returning home to tell her that the 'benefits lady' had recommended that they would get even more benefits if they were divorced but still living together, and later, that if they sold their house they would get more benefits, I could see a further deception that she had not yet properly grasped – that her assets were being systematically stripped. Should I open up this topic and risk inflicting new pain, or not highlight this issue? It seemed that her desire to understand what had been going on was paramount to her, despite the pain, so this was an issue we did explore.

'For the first time in my life I had a panic attack,' said Christine at the start of our third session. 'It was really horrid.' It had happened straight after our second session but paradoxically she felt this marked the turning point for her recovery. What she seemed to be saying was that for the first time she had really faced the enormity of her situation, which had been overwhelming. However, it had allowed her to start properly processing the hurt.

By session five she felt she had put '90 per cent of the jigsaw together' and by session seven suspected that the physical pains she had experienced were actually an expression of her mental pain. Focusing on her emotional life had been so out of character for her that she could only see physical illness as the route into therapy. She asked me, 'If it hadn't come out with the [physical] pain, how else could it come out?'

Later in therapy, she admitted, 'I don't feel as confused as I did when I first came. My mind was like snakes sliding round one another. I still can't get round the degree of his deceit.' She felt that the time had come to drop the preoccupation with her husband and move on. Although she could not forgive him, she could forget and lay the matter to rest. We negotiated how best to 'move on' and emerged with an unusual solution. I went out of the therapy office and came back with the biggest book I had in the house – *The Chronicle of Great Britain*. She was pleased because she also had this book. She sat with the book on her lap and then with a bang closed it as hard as she could. This symbolized 'closing the episode', and that is exactly what she did.

In the following session she reported that she had stopped her painkillers, stopped drinking half a bottle of brandy a day, enjoyed reading two daily newspapers, felt 'clear-headed', resumed her college course and said there was no need for any hip injections because she didn't have osteoarthritis after all. She now described what had been physical pain as 'discomfort' that returned only at times of stress. She said, 'This is the first time I've had peace of mind for forty years.'

Before psychological therapy, Christine McKenzie had not been able to consciously acknowledge and express her profound emotional pain; the expression of her pain was literal, somatic, in bodily aches and pains. It involved endless visits to doctors, specialists' clinics and hospitals, had received a semi-medical label, 'fibromyalgia', and was treated without avail, with many medications. Christine remained confused and could not find the peace of mind that eluded her. What had happened to make her emotional pain into an illness? And why is the medical illness route more acceptable and accessible within the NHS?

The illness of the NHS

Although the NHS may be neatly divided into body (medical specialists) and mind (psychiatry, psychology and counselling) solutions, human beings do not divide up into neat mind–body categories. Psychological and physical functions share the same one body, and the bodily pathways involved in emotions and illness are often identical. For instance, the raised blood pressure, heart rate and temperature when someone is acutely anxious operate within the same blood vessels and heart that can be affected by heart disease. The stomach churning, indigestion and diarrhoea that may accompany worry operate in the same gastric system as does a bacterial infection. Emotions are not solely mental or occupying some non-physical space, but are firmly linked with the body. The possibilities for overlap and confusion are very great, particularly if the person is not aware of the link between psychological events and emotion. The bodily aspects of emotions may easily be misinterpreted in terms of physical illness.

Not only that, but there is accumulating evidence that continuous stress, anxiety, depression and anger increase the risk of developing many different physical conditions and diseases. Stress has been shown to lower immune function,[1] slow the rate of wound healing,[2] diminish the effectiveness of vaccines,[3] reduce the gene expression of growth hormone in blood cells,[4] induce DNA damage,[5] and affect the accuracy of DNA repair.[6] In a review of negative emotions and health, Tracy Mayne, Director of HIV Epidemiology at the New York City Department of Health, concluded that 'the research supporting the hypothesis that frequent intense negative affect can directly damage the body is overwhelming'.[7] The physical pathways by which continuous negative emotions could produce medical disorders include excessive cardiovascular arousal,[8] hormone change,[9] changes in brain chemistry,[10] physiological over-arousal,[11] and immune dysregulation of inflammatory responses.[12] Conversely, there is also evidence that feelings of pleasure and well-being are predictors of good health in future years. It would appear that there is a strong interaction between emotions and health or disease.[13]

The overlap between emotions and illness is nowhere more evident than in the GP surgery. One area of developing research is in 'medically unexplained symptoms'. This is when patients are suffering from physical pain or discomfort for which no medical illness or organic causes can be found. It has been estimated that between 15 and 30 per cent of all consultations with a GP are for 'medically unexplained symptoms'.[14,15] Researchers at Guy's, King's College and St Thomas' Hospital, London, have also followed up hospital outpatient attendees in eleven NHS Trusts in 2001 and found 27 per cent had a medically explained episode.[16] The GP John McCormack put it like this: 'All your tests are negative, Mrs Jones, therefore you have no oro/neuro/endocrino/otorhinalaryngo/respiro/rheumato/opthalmdo/reno/physio/psycho-logical problem.'[17] The patient is then discharged, sometimes relieved that they 'have nothing', but more often perplexed because they are sure something is not right. Alternatively, they are sent to another speciality where new tests are repeated. Sometimes they go round and round the different hospital departments. Many GPs operate adeptly with this daily mind–body confusion, often opting for physical solutions. One GP I know, who trained first as a clinical psychologist, admitted that she often knew the problem was emotional but did not have time to ask the crucial question, 'What has been happening in your life?', knowing a Pandora's box would be opened. Giving a pill for the physical symptoms is often the easy solution.

Early steps towards illness

Kirsty's first week at school was a kaleidoscope experience for her. She had not mixed much with other children, mainly staying at home with her mother. Now everyone spoke so loudly, so quickly, and the other children shot their hands in the air when teacher asked a question, and there seemed so many new things to do. But one thing Kirsty knew about was drawing. She often coloured things with her felt-tip pens and copied pictures from magazines. Kirsty's home life was the key to understanding why school was so overwhelming. Since her birth Kirsty's mother had suffered from postnatal depression and chronic fatigue. She used to keep the lights low, and the TV volume down because it seemed so piercing and oppressive. When Kirsty was a baby she could not bear to hear crying and either left her for long periods to cry or else relied on Bob, Kirsty's father, to do something. Bob was usually at a loss at what to do and, anyway, over the years was absent from home life for longer and longer periods. Kirsty's mum tried to carry on as best she could, but was so preoccupied she did not respond to Kirsty as well as she might. Conversation was minimal, as were tender moments of loving, and catching baby's eye, trying to make her laugh and giggle. What seemed to hold Kirsty's mum together were her weekly visits to her GP, Dr Donovan, who would attend to her medical regime, adjusting the dosage of antidepressants, tranquillizers and sleeping tablets to help her achieve some sort of equilibrium.

That morning, Kirsty had produced a beautiful multicoloured picture of a fairground scene – she copied it from a picture on the classroom wall. Miss Ingle had praised her abundantly, as Miss Ingle was apt to do with all her pupils, but there was no smile on Kirsty's face, no recognition that she was pleased with being praised. If we were able to feel what Kirsty felt we would be surprised too. She felt very little – she did not know what to feel. She was unused to praise, actually unused to anything quite as noisy as Miss Ingle, and was more perplexed than anything else.

'You must take that home to Mummy,' Miss Ingle insisted. 'She will love it.' Kirsty could not remember her mother being enthusiastic at anything much she had done and did not expect a reaction. But Miss Ingle said so, and Kirsty would do it.

'Here, Mummy,' Kirsty said, showing it to her mother. 'It's a fair.' Her mother looked at it, knew she should respond to her child, and said, 'It's beautiful, dear,' like she had seen mothers do in the TV 'soaps' she often watched. But although the words were right, her eyes did not sparkle, her voice showed little intonation, and her body was rather stiff as she handed the picture back. She had behaved correctly, she thought, but felt no spontaneous happiness. Similarly, Kirsty felt no pleasure; it had not been as Miss Ingle had said it would be, and the phrase 'She will love it' kept reverberating in her mind. She had the idea that something, somewhere, was not right. In fact the clash between home life and school was so extreme that Kirsty had an uneasy idea that maybe a whole lot of things were not right, but she could never have described these thoughts.

That night, Kirsty experienced a churning stomach, racing heart and breathing difficulties. She screamed out, and this time her mother came to help. Her mother spent several hours with her, checking her pulse and giving her doses of Calpol. She kept saying, 'Tomorrow we must go and see Dr Donovan', and that is exactly what happened. Dr Donovan examined Kirsty carefully and could not find anything amiss, but noting her mother's insistence that something should be done, prescribed 10 mg of Buscopan, three times a day, told her mother to keep her in bed with plenty of liquids and come back to him if matters worsened. Mother nursed Kirsty until she was well, and three days later she went back to school.

The somatic focus

Kirsty's emotional education was sadly impoverished. Lacking stimulation and response from her mother meant that she could not easily understand and tune into her own emotional life, nor the emotions of others. She knew something was wrong when she came across the stark contrast of life at school, but did not know what to feel or how to express it. When her mother failed to praise her like Miss Ingle said she would, her body reacted, but she had no way of understanding this, no words for 'disappointment', and no sense that this feeling was the direct result of mother's inadequate response. The bodily sensations remained, though: she felt a churning stomach, which was unusual for her, and she cried out. Her mother's concerned reaction was comforting and confirmed the idea of a stomach illness. The experience with Dr Donovan, her three days off school and further attention from mother helped to label the episode as 'illness' rather than 'emotion'. During her childhood there were many visits to Dr Donovan, many medications, and mother found it easier to react to her illnesses than respond to relationship issues. In her upbringing Kirsty failed to develop a proper understanding of her emotional life, but became increasingly aware of the somatic symptoms of anxiety without an understanding of their psychological meaning and context.[18]

Even today, after an argument with her husband, Kirsty is crippled with stomach pains, for which she has plenty of medications, and watches her diet, vitamin and mineral intake with excessive care. She is only dimly aware that her pains have anything to do with her relationship with her husband, and anyway avoids confrontation whenever she can. Her husband finds it impossible to understand why she has had so many hospital investigations and visits to the GP for her persistent stomach, heart, and breathing problems. He tries hard to avoid 'upsetting' her. Kirsty has developed what we might call a 'somatic' reaction to life's stresses and strains. This puts her at a real disadvantage in emotionally processing stressful life events. Her gaze is so rarely turned towards significant emotional issues that she has not got her foot on the first rung of the ladder for beginning the work of emotional processing. The medical profession, hospital visits, medical assessments, alternative therapists, medications, vitamins, natural remedies and literature on new diets and therapies all feed into an unhealthy somatic orientation to life. They seem to shout the message that 'You need to be careful with your health; you could easily come down with something', which, strangely enough, were exactly the words that her mother had often used.

Ruminating Your Life Away

Deadly inheritance

It seemed to Rowena that her life had been a garden of happiness until that single day when her fortunes turned so dramatically. 'Mother passed away peacefully last night at 4.00 a.m.,' said her brother Graham over the phone to Rowena at her house in Windermere.

'Was Morag there?' Rowena enquired [Rowena's elder sister].

'No, she never made it in time… it caught us all as a bit of a surprise.'

'Well, I wish you'd at least have told me that it was getting close.'

Rowena's grief was a strange, mixed-up affair. She was, of course, extremely sad for the loss of her mother, but really regretted that she had never managed to get close to her mother in her last years. She was angry with Graham too, who, with his wife Mary, lived with, and looked after Mother, in her house in Eastbourne. He had a closeness to Mother that she had never had, and Rowena often felt he was keeping her to himself, keeping her away. Had he purposely informed her older sister and kept her in the dark?

It was when she was later told the arrangements for the funeral that she became most upset. Apparently Morag, as the eldest child, had been appointed as sole executor. She had at least expected to be co-executor as the second oldest child and having a degree in Economics and Business Studies. She was also by far the most financially successful, though she did not like to embarrass her brother and sister with this.

The funeral itself was deeply moving and a chance to get closer to friends and family. Rowena's annoyance at Graham and Morag was very much secondary to the grief and family solidarity of the day. It was when Rowena heard about her mother's will that the deepest hurt, and the one that still reverberates today, was made. She could not believe that Mother had stipulated that Graham and his wife could permanently reside in her house as long as they needed to – even for life! Hadn't she realized that in effect Mother had robbed Morag and Rowena of their inheritance? Graham wasn't the greatest for initiative and it was more than likely he'd just stay on until he died too. True, Mother's section of her pretty large house could be rented off and the proceeds of the rent split between her and Morag, but how could that compensate for the substantial sum that would be realized by the current sale of Mother's house?

Rowena was on the phone to Graham straight away. 'I assume you will be doing the right thing and moving out quite soon,' she suggested to a rather bemused Graham, who had not given the matter any thought. Graham didn't really know what to think but suggested talking to Morag, 'because she is the one with the know-how', which is exactly what Rowena did. She was shocked, hurt and offended when Morag, usually pretty mild and easy going, said, 'It was mother's wish and I don't think it would be right to overrule her wishes.'

'But, I mean, how compos mentis was she in her last few months?' Rowena added.

'Oh, she made her will years ago,' Morag replied. That really sealed it – all this subterfuge behind her back, and no one had seen fit to tell her about a will made years ago. If Rowena had known she could have explained to Mother about the financial flaws in this arrangement. Mother would have seen that straight away, she was sure.

And now, sitting on her veranda looking out over the lake fifteen years later, the issue still burns on in Rowena's mind. Every morning as she sits there with her coffee, it would seem that she still had to swallow the same bitter emotional pill. Why had Graham been so unreasonable? Had they been in it together – denying her what was altogether just and reasonable? How could Mother have been so taken in? Actually she had found in the latter years that she rarely had any fond feelings towards Mother. When she thought of her it was more with perplexity and a feeling of being misunderstood than with love. She tried to fathom out whether the whole affair was based on misunderstandings or whether they had purposely planned it this way.

Every morning her stomach churned and her muscles tensed as she relived the sense of injustice, anger and foolishness of it all. Once she even snapped the handle of the coffee mug in two as she clenched her fist. She had gone over it again and again and again, day in, day out, re-experiencing those hurts every day, sometimes even waking from sleep to turn it over in her mind.

She had argued a few times with Graham and lost contact over the years. Even when he eventually sold the house and each party did receive a handsome share (house prices had risen steeply since her mother's death), it did not seem to break the sense of bitterness and betrayal. Graham had hoped this would win back his sister's affection, but the cut seemed too deep for Rowena.

Rowena hoped that every morning as she sat by the lakeside she would think on more peaceful things, but without fail her thoughts and emotions would follow the same treadmill. She had occasionally referred to this daily 'rest period' as a time for 'working through her problem', but anyone with the power to observe thoughts, as a birdwatcher observes birds from a hide, would have seen exactly the same pattern of thoughts, arriving day after day and year after year in the same sequence and with the same pattern.

Does ruminating resolve anything?

One of the main attributes of emotional processing emphasized in the 'Healing through Feeling' section of this book (Part III) is that facing difficult emotional memories is central to the healing of emotional memories. Yet for fifteen years Rowena had apparently faced the same emotional hurts and memories every day, but without any effective healing, resolution or emotional processing taking place. What was wrong here? What is it about rumination that can block effective healing? And this is what Rowena was doing – ruminating – from the same root as ruminants, which 'chew the cud' for hours every day. It refers to the frequent replaying of the thoughts and memories of some significant emotional event.

One of the features of this is that, with each replaying, powerful emotions are invoked, so that, in a way it is a mini-experience of the original hurt. It can get elaborated over time, as, for instance, in Rowena's case, she began to feel it was a conspiracy, and even implicated her mother in this, which she had not done previously. Rumination takes place in the imagination, but the replay of the emotions releases many of the same biochemical neurotransmitters and physiological processes which occurred in the original emotional event. Rumination does not just apply to anger, but anxiety, depression, jealousy and other emotions too. Nor is it just related to negative emotions: it could involve the replay of exciting, achieving, proud or pleasurable events in one's life.

Rumination over emotional events is absolutely normal. Ninety five per cent of people report having spontaneously ruminated about important emotional events in their lives,[1] and 40 per cent said they have experienced this often or very often. Also, mentally replaying the original incident is a normal element in the emotional processing of a difficult event. So when does rumination become *mal*-adaptive, and when does it hinder emotional processing instead of being a normal constituent part of processing?

On 18 November 1987 a horrific flash fire ripped through the escalators and ticket hall of King's Cross tube station, killing thirty people. Earlier in the year there had been the Zebrugge disaster, in which the *Herald of Free Enterprise* ferry had rolled over and sunk, drowning 200 passengers and crew in the North Sea. This first disaster raised awareness of disaster planning and counselling for post-traumatic stress in Psychiatry and Psychology Departments throughout the UK. A number of private companies were being set up specifically to supply 'trauma debriefing' for businesses and services with a high risk of encountering accidents, such as fire, ambulance and police services. So by the time of the King's Cross disaster in November, many agencies were aware of the need for trauma debriefing. Too aware, it seems. One study estimated that surviving victims at King's Cross were swamped by up to thirty-two different helping agencies.

'Why counselling may make your nightmares even worse', announced the *Daily Mail* on 3 March 2003 after a controlled trial of trauma debriefing had demonstrated that it was ineffective and sometimes harmful for trauma victims. The *Mail* got it slightly wrong in that counselling in general has been shown to be effective, but not when applied immediately after a trauma, as in trauma debriefing. In order to emotionally process events in life it is not just a matter of facing and talking about the event, but facing and talking about it at the right time. Immediately after a trauma is not the right time to be exploring and discussing one's emotional pain. First, the memory of the trauma needs to be registered and consolidated before any discussion or 'working through' of issues can be contemplated. It is here that rumination naturally has a part to play. In registering and initially making sense of what has happened, the trauma victim will probably need to think the situation through over and over again. It is not that they rationally choose to think about it, though – more that they cannot stop thinking about it at first. This would be a normal and healthy phase of emotional processing. If they are still doing this nine months later, the rumination has not resulted in any effective emotional processing and has become stuck in an unproductive groove.

Getting under the skin

Under what circumstances would it be normal to ruminate about emotional events? National disasters, or personal disasters and accidents in which a person's life and safety are threatened are so intense, so personal, and burst the 'it won't ever happen to me' bubble, that the rumination on the traumatic event is inevitable. According to the Belgian psychologists Pierre Philippot and Bernard Rimé, who had conducted extensive research on rumination, the stronger, more intense and more personal the emotional hurt, the greater is the need for:

> '... longer and more effortful regulation processes (rumination). Because of their emotionality and their implication for the individual's concerns, the trace of the event in autobiographical memory should be stronger and more easily activated. Ultimately, these events should be re-evoked more often, and the re-evocation should yield strong emotions.'[2]

So the intensity of the hurt is crucial. But what is 'intense'? Disasters and traumas are universally intense, but they are not the only type of intense emotional event. What is intense or 'gets under the skin' of one person may not be the same as for another.

Johnny had had a serious childhood bike accident, which entailed several painful operations and being in traction for six weeks in hospital. When he damaged his knee in a minor car accident at age forty-three, this proved to be a particularly intense experience for him, reverberating with so many unpleasant memories from the past. On the other hand, his friend Wayne, who had often been humiliated in class for being a 'thicko', was not too upset when he had a minor car accident, but any hint from his superiors at work that he was not up to the job would set off ruminations, sweats and sleepless nights in which he tried to grapple with the feelings of shame and inadequacy. Everyone has their own unique and personal memories that partly help explain what fuels some events with their intensity.

In the 'Love and Pasta' chapter (Chapter 10) I described emotional schemas, in which certain emotional understandings coloured a person's current perceptions of events. Earlier in this chapter I described how Rowena's failure to inherit what she felt was rightfully hers was such a powerful and devastating emotional event for her because it slotted into an important schema about an 'unfairness' that had developed from childhood onwards. Rowena had been jealous of her older sister and strove to be as intelligent and attractive as her. On the other hand, Graham, the 'baby of the family', attracted more love and cosseting from Mother than she did, which seemed grossly unfair. Ideas of achievement and unfairness grew and become a predominant theme in her emotional life so that she began to interpret even quite neutral things, like Graham getting a nice birthday present, as unfair. As she grew up, she did not leave the schema behind her in childhood, but tended to 'read' situations with her teenage friends, and later her boyfriends and her husband, Alan (whom she subsequently divorced), in the same way. The matter of the inheritance evoked a powerful emotional schema, making this 'slight' into a nuclear bomb of an event.

Another reason why some emotional events may be particularly intense for a person is that they threaten their 'precious', to use an analogy from *The Lord of the Rings*; that is, those things in their identity and personality that are especially meaningful to them – intellectual freedom, good looks, physical prowess, financial security, independence, being loved, health, social standing and so on. Whatever is personally meaningful to them, if assaulted by circumstances or the actions of others, often engenders intense emotional pain and hurt. The deeper the hurt, the more likely it is that 'longer and more effortful regulation processes' of rumination will occur, to use the words of Philippot and Rimé.

Sometimes events that are normally tolerated quite well seem for some inexplicable reason to affect the person more deeply than usual. This may be related less to personality, identity or schemas, but more to periods of personal stress. When an individual is under stress, their resilience will be lower. Mood is especially affected with a susceptibility to feeling anxious, sad or angry. This tendency to overreact emotionally, to be more emotionally responsive to hurts and slights than normal, is often summed up in the psychological term 'emotional lability'. Few people are immune from the effects of stress. If a significant emotional event occurs during a time of increased stress, the impact on the person will be much greater, with more rumination.

Conundrum

The 'Healing through Feeling' section of this book shows how problems such as alcoholism, phobias, memories of trauma, grief and obsessional thoughts can be healed by facing the hurt. Yet in rumination the person experiences the hurt thousands of times. So why then doesn't emotional pain diminish? This question gets at the heart of how emotional processing works. Returning to the diagram of how emotions operate (see Figure 6, page 140), the ruminative sequence of thoughts and memories (input event) simply re-kindle the original emotion without effective resolution.

By looking at the differences between psychological therapy and chronic rumination, we can understand what is *not* helpful in rumination. Philippot and Rimé discuss the difference between psychological therapy and sharing with a friend or

Figure 6: The ruminative loop

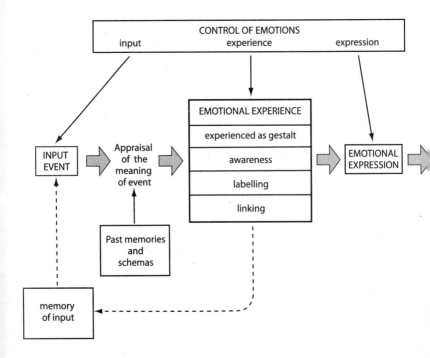

confidante. They feel that this natural sharing with a friend lacks the depth that may come with a therapist. For instance, a young mother who feels disgust towards her new baby may find this stigmatizing to share with a friend, but may not have the same problem with an independent and confidential therapist. But generally, sharing is important and differs dramatically from the act of rumination as the table (*right*) shows.

A number of different psychotherapy researchers suggest that the key element in effective emotional processing is that new information is incorporated into the emotional sequence[3] so that there is a 'reconstruction rather than a repetition'.[4]

How therapy/sharing and rumination differ

Therapy/Sharing	Rumination
Externally steered	Self-steered
New ideas, viewpoints, thought patterns and solutions can be introduced.	Rigidly sticks to the same patterns
Repetitive cycles can be disrupted – not allowing the same emotion to be rekindled	Cycles continue to the end – the same emotion is rekindled
Therapist can steer towards unresolved emotions	Person can avoid 'troublespots' and allow self-deception
Resolution possible	Resolution not usually achieved
Keep anchored on one thing	Flitting
Can focus on one emotion	Other emotions can be added to elaborate and strengthen rumination
New information introduced to emotional appraisal	No new information introduced
Beliefs can be invalidated	Beliefs rarely change
Long exposure times	Short exposure, moving on to the next thought at will
Habituation/decay of troublesome emotion	Sensitization – increased emotional hurt
Emotion expressed	Emotion not outwardly expressed
There is external action (speaking or doing)	There is no external action – it all takes place in the imagination

The sequence of processing described in the 'Healing through Feeling' section involves facing and experiencing the emotion, expressing it and resolving it. At an early stage, rumination may help the person in understanding and resolving issues, and lead to action. For instance, Rowena could have met with her brother and sister and tried to talk the issue through, or, alternatively, tried to understand Graham's point of view, or even forgive him. If the early rumination leads to no resolution, then an entrenched pattern may set in which is simply self-perpetuating.[5]

Vicious circles

'Meta-cognition' is the name of a process in which a person experiences emotion about emotions. It is another aspect of rumination. For instance, a person might become angry about being depressed, anxious about being depressed, depressed about being anxious or almost any combination.

In one of the Emotional Processing courses that I ran with counsellors Ann Henderson and Sandra May, we explained how crying was part of nature's healing process; how it involved facing the hurt, and expressing it in a healthy way; that this followed a time-limited course in which distress reached a crescendo of sobbing, followed by a calm as the crying receded. One of the course participants, Tara, replied that 'I could cry for England' and went on to describe the experience of being bullied at work, after which the crying did not reach a natural crescendo followed by relief. She said, 'I cried all day and all night – I had puffy eyes, and felt washed out and couldn't sleep. I didn't feel any better at the end of it, only worse.'

I asked her what emotion she had added to the sadness and tears. It took some time to identify this, but feelings of recrimination and self-blame were a major schema for Tara. In her childhood she was made responsible for her mother's reckless behaviour while drunk and gradually she had assumed the mantle of responsibility for other members of the family, and later for almost anyone else too. The emotion she added to her tears was self-blame. She blamed herself for feeling down, for being so stupid for allowing herself to get bullied again, and for crying so much. This amounted to a vicious cycle in which the self-blame kept the tears going, causing more self-blame, then more tears, and so on.

In my previous book, *Understanding Panic Attacks and Overcoming Fear*,[6] I described another pernicious type of vicious cycle in which the same emotion fed off itself. In panic attacks, a bodily sensation such as feeling palpitations may make the person afraid (often a fear they might have a heart attack), which increases the speed of the palpitations, confirming the fear ('This really is a heart attack this time'), increasing palpitations in a vicious cycle.

Likewise, if a person feels low, they may have depressing thoughts such as 'Oh no, this is the beginning of another period of depression', making them feel lower, with thoughts such as 'This downward spiral will lead to me committing suicide', leading to more depressed feelings towards a lower and lower ebb. 'Self-focused attention' has been linked to other conditions, such as alcoholism, and is regarded as a general vulnerability factor for a whole variety of psychological dysfunctions.[7]

Downward spirals are also very relevant to physical disorders and the development of chronic illness. In 1992, Barkski introduced the concept of 'amplification' to explain how focusing on a bodily tension magnified the tension further in a deteriorating vicious cycle.[8,9] The psychologist Timothy Sharp also applied this to real physical pain. He suggested that worry about pain causes a person to become hyper-vigilant to pain sensations, which amplifies the pain and also 'primes fear mechanisms'.[10]

These types of closed circuit habits of thinking and feeling have similarities to rumination. Above all, if they continue for any time they increase distress, are disruptive, and being inner-focused take the person away from productive action and involvement in the real world.

Finally...

In the final section of *Emotional Processing: Healing through Feeling*, I have focused on three barriers that can impede the processing of emotional hurts: negative emotional schemas, a somatic focus and rumination. If that is what should not be done, what about what should be done? How can distressing emotions be handled better? Is there a right way to control or regulate feelings? Can a person facilitate the 'dissolving of distress'? I shall go on to explore these important issues and ask the puzzling question: is there any such thing as a right balance in emotional life?

Living in Harmony with Emotions

Who is healthier?

It was the big day for Billy. He had been having driving lessons for six months, and now his driving test was here. Billy had been scouring the showrooms and had lined up a smart blue Nissan 200 SX Turbo sports car he had seen locally. He had asked the salesman to reserve it for him, and saved enough for the deposit. That weekend, it would be his. The driving test was a routine bit of red tape; naturally he would pass.

During the test he went through all the manoeuvres, reasonably enough, he thought, although his mind was more on the blue Turbo sports car than the irritating and, he considered, infantile exercises he was asked to complete. When the test was over, the tester asked Billy to park the car and switch off the engine. He turned to Billy and said, 'I'm afraid, Mr Caldwell, on this occasion I am not going to pass you,' and was about to explain the reasons when Billy shouted, 'What the f– are you talking about?' accusing him of 'f– picking on me from the moment I got into the car.' He screwed up the document the bewildered instructor had given him, got out of the car, slammed the door, kicked the car and, still fuming, headed for home. Bursting in the front door, he searched the house for his mother, finally locating her upstairs. He swore at her, saying, 'Why didn't you buy me more driving lessons? What's wrong with you?

You should have known that f– instructor would fail me. What does he know about driving anyway?'

Karen had often wondered whether the 'falling in love' thing could ever happen to her and had been really surprised on meeting Shaun. Even before she had got used to the idea that someone could love her so passionately, Shaun had been involved in a terrible accident, leaving him with incapacitating brain damage. The compensating joy for Karen was later to discover that she was pregnant. Sadly, this second dream was also shattered when she miscarried. But Karen has not shared her distress with her university friends, Shaun's friends and family who live nearby, or her own family. She has not consulted the university counselling service nor her own GP. For months on end she has sat alone in her flat, only just able to continue her university course, and she has not shed a single tear. Today is the day she had been given for the baby's birth. As she recollects what was and what might have been, she sighs. The sigh is the one observable sign of her grief and despair.

Who is the healthier? Karen, who expressed no more than a sigh, or Billy, who, should we say, expressed himself rather clearly? When I relate these two imaginary scenarios in session five of the Emotional Processing course and ask the question, 'Who is healthier?' occasionally the answer is 'Billy, because he let his feelings out', but usually the answer is 'Neither'. Karen has not expressed her grief and upset, nor tried to understand exactly what it is she is feeling. She has not reached towards identifying the repeated devastation of the raising, and then the loss, of hope. She manages to maintain her university course work, just, but she is not concentrating properly; once a bright, achieving student, she is now quiet and dull. Billy, on the other hand, is still spitting flames at (a) the tester, (b) his mother, (c) his driving school, (d) the system, (e) the car in which he did the test: in fact everyone apart from himself. So in terms of psychological and physical health, who is the healthier?

Billy may have discharged his feelings through his direct expression of anger, but did this 'get rid of' his anger? Carol Tarvis, a social psychologist, has written extensively on anger. In 'On the Wisdom of Counting to Ten: Personal and Social Dangers of Anger Expression',[1] she criticizes psychologists for cultivating the belief that letting anger 'all hang out' is healthy. She lists the unhelpful aspects of direct expression of anger as:

- escalation of the conflict
- making a bad situation worse
- emotional distance as a result of misunderstanding
- miscommunication with the target of one's anger
- rehearsal of grievances
- acquiring a hostile disposition
- losing self-esteem
- feeling *more* tense, and *more* angry
- raised blood pressure.

Even if Billy felt relieved at having 'got his feelings out', his aggressive frame of mind would lead him to appraise many situations in a hostile manner, just as Terry did (see Chapter 10). It is likely that Billy is easily stirred up to anger, and regularly has a great deal more anger to 'get rid of' than most people. His tantrum is only a temporary outflow of a river being constantly filled by new tributaries of anger.

Where anger and medicine meet

A major analytic review of forty-five studies of hostility and physical health conducted at the University of Texas Medical Branch showed that after controlling other risk factors, hostility was a significant risk for coronary heart disease.[2] Another study at Berkeley University and Finnish universities showed that hostility was related to an increased risk of myocardial infarction (heart attack),[3] and a further study showed that hostility predicted sickness and ill health absences in a large workforce.[4] Persistent anger is thought to increase the risk of heart disease by increasing blood pressure and damaging blood vessel walls.[5]

What about Karen? Could her life be threatened by her extreme failure to express emotions? By not allowing herself to think about, talk about, or express her feelings in any way, it is unlikely that Karen could properly label and understand her feelings, much less face them and work through them. Emotional processing would be impeded. Possibly, like Christine (in Chapter 11), her bodily distress might be manifested in physical, somatic symptoms rather than finding emotional expression. Her current tendency to avoid thinking about her feelings, holding them in, generally slowing down and not fully engaging in the world, is part of a what is often regarded as a depressive reaction.

In controlled research studies, depression has been linked to increased risk of myocardial infarction,[6] coronary artery disease,[7] cancer,[8] and, in the elderly, lowered bone mineral density[9] and decline in muscle strength.[10] Currently, Karen is locked into a position where her distress has no outlet, and it is likely to be taking a psychological or physical toll on her body.

The German psychologist Ronald Grossarth-Matisek conducted a large-scale longitudinal health survey in Yugoslavia, in which the inhabitants of the small town of Cruenka (14,000 people) were medically followed up over a period of 21 years.[11] One of the factors measured in the first survey (1965) was the degree to which individuals held a pro-rational/anti-emotional attitude, that is, 'I do not let emotions influence me in any way.' When the researchers checked deaths from lung cancer in their second survey in 1976, as would be expected, 31 of 674 heavy smokers (more than 20 cigarettes a day) had died. However, when their attitude to emotions (measured in the 1965 survey) was examined, all 31 of those who had died had a highly rational, anti-emotional attitude. Not a single heavy smoker who had had a positive or moderately positive attitude towards emotions in the 1965 survey had died by 1976. This rather unusual finding lends weight to the idea that emotions and physical health are integrally fused together. Returning to Karen and Billy, we could say that research evidence suggests that their extreme patterns of emotional expression ultimately put both of them at risk of physical illness.

The difference between experiencing and expressing emotion

Although in practice the experience and expression of emotions run into one another, they are different aspects of the emotions cycle. It is possible to allow oneself to fully feel an emotion, such as anger, but to delay or defer expressing it. This is what Carol Tarvis calls 'the wisdom of counting to ten'. Deferring the *expression* of anger does not harm the individual concerned, but stifling the *experience* could initially be problematic because it removes an important source of information; the person may not properly understand what they are feeling, and hence cannot respond appropriately. Several types of expression are possible. Billy's repertoire of abuse and aggression is not particularly conducive to good relationships. He would benefit from learning 'appropriate assertiveness', taught in many 'anger management' groups. This differs from aggressiveness in that the person constructively expresses their point of view, but without the rise in tone and threatening behaviour that generally raises the shutters and closes the ears of the listener. The offended person directly approaches the offender to explain rationally how their behaviour has affected them; this normally implies a delay in time, allowing the first white-hot anger to subside, but nevertheless confronts the issue that triggered the anger.

Can emotions be tamed?

If the extremes of emotional expression are unhealthy, where is the healthy balance? Is there a correct type of emotional

149

expression? Throughout this book I have used many quite extreme examples, where people have suppressed or controlled emotions too much, and I might have given the impression that any control was bad. The psychologist James Gross at Stanford University has written extensively on emotion control, or as he calls it, 'emotions regulation', pointing out that emotional regulation is a normal and healthy part of childhood development and the conduct of an adult.[12,13] But where is the line between healthy and unhealthy control? How can someone beneficially control emotions without impairing their emotional life? Can a right balance be found?

To find the best ways to regulate emotion, it is important to look at the whole emotion cycle. It might be possible to remove distressing emotions by avoiding anything stressful in life

Figure 7: Can emotions be changed?

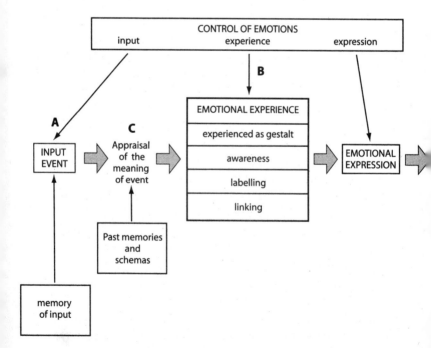

(see Figure 7, point A), such as taking an easy job, not getting into relationships, not having children. Sometimes it is right to avoid or try to change difficult situations, for instance to change jobs if it is unreasonably oppressive, or to take steps to ensure that the workload is reduced. But avoidance can have a sting in the tail because the attempts at avoidance often carry their own different types of stress, such as feelings of underachievement. If avoidance becomes a predominant style of coping, it can seriously restrict the joys and successes of life. We have to look elsewhere in the emotion cycle to find the most healthy patterns of emotion regulation.[14]

The Murphy's Law of emotional experience

At a seaside resort near where I live, a marine experiment is being conducted in the hopes of attracting surfers to the area. They are using banks of shingle out at sea to force the water current through a small inlet, creating powerful artificial waves suitable for surfing. No one knows how successful it will be, and while the proponents of the experiment say it is quite safe, the detractors predict a disastrous impact on other areas of the coast.

Is it possible to somehow channel emotions in a healthier direction? Can this be successful, or, like this surfing experiment, could it have an adverse effect on other areas of the psyche? One panic sufferer described how she attempted to keep on a happy level all the time. She said, 'Before, I wanted everything to be perfect – nearly every day I was wanting to stay on this happy level all the time. I didn't want to appear out of control to anyone else – angry, unhappy – I had this "nothing bothers me" exterior. Now I've come to the regrettable conclusion that ups and down are normal.' In common with many other people she wanted to prolong happy feelings and avoid unhappy ones. Trying to keep a pleasant feeling going is usually pretty unproductive, because the more a person tries, the more the happy experience seems to slip away from them. Happiness, like a butterfly, is elusive. It is the spontaneity, the newness, the excitement that is enjoyable, and spontaneity cannot be kept going perpetually. It just happens, and is best left to its own devices. Studies on 'flow' indicate that when a person is fully absorbed in an activity that they are good at, they 'lose themselves' in the flow; they are so focused on the activity that they cease to be aware of their own needs and feelings and often report these are their happiest moments. The Murphy's Law aspect to all this is that if you are trying to avoid an unpleasant emotional experience it has the nasty habit of following you around and refusing to go away! It's not fair. Try to keep something pleasant and it leaves you. Try to stop something unpleasant and you cannot get rid of it.

In the 1960s, an interesting type of psychological therapy called 'paradoxical intention' was introduced, which sheds light on this Murphy's Law phenomenon. Patients with a particular problem, such as blushing, are encouraged in paradoxical intention to want to blush, to try to blush, in fact to try to do the very thing they have been so assiduously avoiding for years. One of the effects of trying to make the unpleasant experience occur is that it cannot be done. Changing the mindset into one of desiring to do something seems to ruin it. The blushing response just will not happen. The suggestion here is that the dynamics of avoidance are different from those of desire. In avoidance, in order to keep an experience at bay, there must be a level of unconscious monitoring of whether that experience is imminent, in other words, you have to be aware of the unwanted experience all the time in order to spot it and eradicate it.[15,16] This unconscious monitoring means that the unwanted experience is ever-present. It does seem quite perverse that the pursuit of happiness can be elusive, whereas trying to keep misery at bay is doomed.

A willingness to accept the ups and downs of experience, to realize that both joy and sorrow are necessary bedfellows, not to try to mould what is essentially ephemeral, allows a richer and more vital spectrum of experiences to play out their course. This is described well by the psychotherapist Carl Rogers, whom I quoted in Chapter 4, on the openness needed to 'become the person I really am':

> 'There is a gradual growth of trust in, and even an affection for, the complex, rich, varied assortment of feelings and tendencies which exist [in the person] at the organic level. Consciousness, instead of being a watchman over a dangerous and unpredictable lot of impulses, of which few can be permitted to see the light of day, becomes the comfortable inhabitant of a society of impulses, satisfactorily self-governing when not fearfully guarded.'[17]

So, returning to Figure 7, point B (see page 150), it would appear that trying to directly modify, change, force or control the emotional experience aspect of the cycle is not the most productive method of emotional regulation.

The hard and easy way to change emotion

Having pointed towards the importance of fundamentally accepting one's own emotional experience, it does not mean that any attempt of regulation is wrong. Although it may be counterproductive to try to modify emotional experience directly, there are other aspects of the emotion cycle that can be more easily changed, making a difference to our health and happiness. This section looks at the hard and easy way to bring about change.

'I wouldn't be sitting here today if it wasn't for that stupid Julie girl,' Natasha shared with me at the start of our therapy session. She moved uncomfortably in the chair as if to remind us both that her painful back was all Julie's fault.

'So, although you seem to have got over the fear and trauma of the car accident, you have not got over your feelings of anger towards Julie?' I summarized.

'Yes, I seem to be angry all the time now. Whenever my mind turns to the crash, it's always Julie, stupid Julie. I try not to think about her, I try not to be angry, start doing the ironing or hoovering, or anything to take my mind off it, but somehow or other I always seem to end up thinking of her.'

'Should we concentrate on that anger today, then?'

'I'd like to get over it, but I don't see how,' Natasha shared rather honestly.

Natasha had not coped well after her car accident two years before. Her back and shoulder problems had led to a series of small operations, numerous assessments, and three lengthy medical reports as part of her compensation claim. Her high-profile job selling properties overseas had suffered, as had her home life with her husband Jack and their two teenage children. A psychological report commissioned by her solicitors indicated that she was suffering from post-traumatic stress disorder, and I had been asked to supply the psychological treatment to help her overcome this. In our first seven sessions she had done exceptionally well in facing the memories of the car accident and had overcome the fears, flashbacks and anxiety that had become her everyday experience. Once she had grasped the principle of having to face painful memories she tackled the problem rather like clinching one of her property deals, and now she was surprisingly symptom-free. However, there was one remaining issue that had now taken centre stage, an island of anger in an otherwise clear sea.

Julie had been giving Natasha a lift in her new Audi TT Quattro, and much to Natasha's annoyance kept talking to her – and this is what galled Natasha most – looking at her as she talked and drove. Natasha kept thinking, 'She'll have an accident if she doesn't look at the road', and once she said, 'Look out!' to turn Julie's attention to the road. Natasha could see out of the corner of her eye that there was something stationary ahead, but Julie prattled on, until turning and seeing the stationary car at the last minute, hitting the brake (which turned out to be the accelerator) and swerving out into the oncoming traffic.

Natasha had coped with many of the physical problems resulting from the accident, but psychologically speaking, what had haunted her most was the cyclist, an old man who had been sauntering along on his bike. Her flashbacks were nearly always of his terrified look as the car was bearing down on him and the crunching noise as the car hit him and he was catapulted over the bonnet of the car (he survived). Subsequently, their car came to a halt when it hit a van head-on, which was when Natasha injured her back, shoulders and chest. Not only did she blame Julie for the pain and suffering she had experienced, but also for having to suffer the recurring image of the poor cyclist's horrified face.

'But there's nothing I can do to change the way I feel,' Natasha reiterated.

'Tell me about Julie,' I asked.

Apparently Julie had had a number of accidents, and each time her wealthy father had bailed her out (that made Natasha angry too). He had set Julie up as manager in a series of designer dress shops, all of which had failed due to Julie's ineptitude. Julie was very pleasant and sociable with customers but had no idea when it came to running a business. Natasha told me about Julie's annoying habit of asking the same question three times, forgetting appointments, having to write down everything in order to retain it, and using the wrong words in conversation.

It was at this point that I explained the notion of IQ being a bell-shaped distribution, where 100 represents the population average, with very high scores representing genius and very low scores, 'learning difficulties'. Instead of seeing Julie's appalling driving habits and her lack of concern for her victims as selfish, callous, and done on purpose, Natasha began to re-frame Julie as having severe learning difficulties and being buoyed up by her rich and indulgent father. The effect of reconstructing Julie's personality and intentions was incredible. Over the next ten minutes of discussion about dyslexia and cognitive disability, Natasha ceased to blame Julie, and even expressed some sympathy as she recalled previous inexplicable encounters with Julie, which, in the light of her intellectual deficit, now seemed to make sense.

At the next session, Natasha was a changed woman. Her anger had dissipated completely, she had not thought much about the accident, had had a great fortnight with her family, and she was making plans for both her business and a family holiday.

The hard way to change an emotion is the 'It's no good closing the stable door after the horse has bolted' method. Trying to eradicate, modify, pacify or change a powerful emotion once it has started seems at times to be like scaling an impenetrable wall. Returning to Figure 7 (see page 150), point B is the point at which the stable door is closed. This is not usually effective. However, changing the appraisal that underpins the emotion can change the emotional experience (see Figure 7, point C). It is not so easy to identify appraisals, as they are usually rapid, unconscious, self-evidently correct perceptions of reality, rather than 'appraisals' of reality, and may be part of more general, fixed emotional schemas. Natasha had the benefit of sharing her thoughts with another person (who happened to be a therapist), and receiving feedback that helped her to re-examine her appraisal of Julie from 'purposely negligent' to having 'learning difficulties'. The Roman emperor Marcus Aurelius rather radically expressed this 'easy way' in around AD 160, when he said, 'If you are distressed by anything external, the pain is not due to the thing itself, but to your estimate of it; and this you have the power to revoke at any moment.'

For most people this over-simplifies reality, but it does express the idea that the 'appraisal' phase of the emotion cycle is amenable to modification.

All this suggests that one key to emotional health is to develop less critical and more generous estimations of the motives of others and of oneself. It may be necessary to step one stage further back to identify any general negative emotional schema that may pervade one's viewpoint. A negative appraisal of someone in a specific instance may be fed by a generally negative schema about other people. Addressing such a negative schema could help to establish more accurate appraisals of other people's motives.

Healing through feeling

Psychotherapists and counsellors who have striven to help patients come to terms with all manner of distressing life events have for many years implicitly understood the healing potential of emotional processing. This book is the first to formally draw this field together as 'Emotional Processing' and highlight that it encompasses different levels of healing. At one level emotional processing can be seen as a sort of second 'immune system', healing in the sense of absorbing or dissolving life's stresses and restoring emotional equilibrium. Another type of healing is intrinsic to the emotional experience itself, in that all the crucial information about what is troubling the person is contained within the emotion. Understanding or 'reading' the feeling points the way forward. Feelings are honest: you may not feel what you want to feel or ought to feel, but they usually tell the truth. Another level of healing is involved in facing the feeling, instead of avoiding it. Facing feelings ultimately reduces the disturbing power of the emotions, thus opening the door to healing. And the converse is also true. Shutting the psychological gates, suppression, avoidance and other mental mechanisms, can cut off the flow of feeling and hinder any effective understanding and resolution. In one sense, emotional processing could be thought of as an essential part of the body's wisdom – its way of maintaining its emotional equilibrium.

The ultimate offer

At your darkest hour, when you are in distress, where anguish, sadness or pain seem to be your constant partner, when you have forgotten the joy of seeing snowdrops and daffodils and the new life of spring breaking through, when winter seems to last forever, there on the path ahead is a man, a sort of salesman, ready to buy or sell something, to barter with you.

'I can see you are troubled by much distress and are ready to give up,' he begins. 'I can help you with your dilemma.'

'How could you possibly help me?' is your reply.

'I am prepared to take from you every drop of despair, anxiety and anguish. I will take it all and take it forever,' he confidently proclaims as he draws nearer.

'This sounds exactly what I need. I can't go on much longer, feeling like this, it is true. I have never felt so bad in my life, and I would do anything to stop this dreadful feeling.'

'I am your man,' he replies. 'I can do that for you.'

'How can you make it work?' you ask, beginning to feel it is too good to be true.

'In order to make it work,' he continues, 'you must give me all your emotions. Yes, the distress and the anguish, but also the laughter, the fun and happiness. I can't make it work unless you give it all to me and give it all forever. But as you are only feeling constant misery, you won't be missing happy emotions much, will you? I can assure you it will be worth it. No more sadness ever again, no more distress, no more anguish, no more fear, in fact, no more feeling.'

He looks you in the eye. 'So is it a deal then?'

Appendix: The Idea Behind the Science

From behaviour to cognition to emotion

They call it the silver city by the sea. Virtually the whole of the city is built from huge granite blocks taken from a single quarry on the outskirts of Aberdeen. In the sunshine the granite has a sparkle to it, hence 'the silver city'. Aberdeen is on the east coast of Scotland, far enough north to regularly see the aurora borealis – or northern lights, as they are commonly known – during the winter nights. My family lived in a terraced house near the centre of the city, and the Clinical Psychology Department was set in Elmhill House, a fine and imposing granite mansion situated in the grounds of Royal Cornhill Hospital, the main psychiatric hospital in Aberdeenshire.

A large group of clinical psychologists worked from this base – seeing patients with psychological problems, teaching about psychology and coordinating research. We were really a very cohesive group with a particular passion to understand and treat panic attack sufferers. Since leaving Aberdeen I have become accustomed to working in multi-disciplinary teams, so looking back now it does seem a very specialized group. I don't know quite why panic attacks were self-evidently the most important topic to focus on, but they were. It was at a time when psychologists were beginning to feel that behaviour therapy was limited and, like all psychological therapies, had eventually become 'past its sell-by date', and were reaching towards a more cognitive understanding of psychological disorders. It seemed to us that the beliefs patients had about their panic attacks held the secret for understanding and treating the condition successfully. For instance, if a patient believed they would die or be seriously harmed by a panic attack (this is what it feels like) it would in a way be quite reasonable to restrict one's activity to ensure that another attack did not occur. The fault lay in the incorrect belief rather than the avoidant behaviour. The type of therapy we devised and used to help panic sufferers was called 'cognitive invalidation', because the thrust of the therapy was to invalidate the faulty cognition, in this case the belief that a panic attack was dangerous. This approach is outlined in my book *Understanding Panic Attacks and Overcoming Fear*.[1] It is rather odd that in such a 'cognitive' climate the first beginnings of an emotional processing research programme should be stirred.

At that time a number of research studies had shown that the very first panic attack a person experiences often follows from a period of marked stress;[2,3] but what surprised me time and time again in interviewing patients with panic attacks was their failure to link major life stresses, such as a breakdown of their marriage, death of a parent or major operation, with the subsequent experience of their first panic attack.[4] Was it normal, I pondered, to miss the connection between major emotional stresses and the emergence of panic, or is panic so somatic, so much like a heart attack, that the person fails to perceive it as an emotional event? And there was something else, too: emotions seemed to be regarded with great caution. One man said, 'I allow myself to feel something in myself, like sadness, crying. I go so far down. It's bubbling in my eyes, and I try to stop it and shake off what I am thinking. I don't like starting because I get really hysterical. The last time I did, then I ended up punching a wall.' I began to think that these patients were somehow dealing with or 'processing' their emotions in a problematic way, and that this faulty emotional processing might account for the development of their problem.

Was I observing something of emotional significance or forming an exaggerated opinion on the basis of a few cases? So I did what scientists are supposed to do: put it to the test. A research study was designed in which we would ask fifty panic disorder patients who came to our department for therapy to fill in an emotional control questionnaire and other scales indicating how much they understood their emotions. Nearly 200 healthy volunteers from the Aberdeen University Psychology Department were also sent the same questionnaire pack. In this way we were able to compare the replies of the panic patients with those given by healthy adults who did not experience panic. The findings were very clear-cut. The panic patients tried to smother or bottle up feelings of anger, sadness and anxiety to a far greater extent than the healthy volunteers. They were extremely aware of their bodily sensations and emotions but less able to accurately label their emotions.[5] Doctors Maggie Watson and Steven Greer, colleagues at the Royal Marsden Cancer Hospital, who had used the same emotional control questionnaire in comparing a group of cancer patients with a group of healthy, normal individuals, put forward a hypothesis that excessive control of emotions could predispose a person to cancer.[6] This hypothesis was based on an 8 per difference between their two groups, whereas our study showed a 20 per cent difference between the panic sufferers and the healthy volunteers. It seemed I was on the right track, but as in most research, there were more questions at the end than at the beginning!

Not another questionnaire!

I began to wonder whether the suppression or control of emotions created the conditions for a panic attack, or whether this applied to other anxiety conditions too. It then occurred to me that it might be broader still, contributing towards depression or to all psychiatric disorders. Then again there was the question of causality. Could excessive suppression of emotions set off an anxiety condition, or was the faulty processing simply the *result* of having an anxiety condition?

I was also aware of a measurement limitation. We had chosen the emotion questionnaires not so much on the basis of what key emotional dimensions we wanted to measure but rather what emotion questionnaires were available. And at that time there were not many. It reminded me of the story of a drunken man looking for his keys under a streetlight. A stranger stops to help him and after a fruitless five minutes searching says, 'Where exactly did you drop your keys?'

'On the other side of the street,' comes the reply, 'but the light is much better here.'

Apart from all these questions about the link between emotions and psychological problems, I realized by the end of the study that research into emotions could not progress very far without better assessment instruments. Having previously developed an assessment for use with long-stay schizophrenic patients with my psychologist colleague John Hall, called REHAB (Rehabilitation Evaluation Hall And Baker),[7] which had proved valuable in the rehabilitation of long-stay psychiatric patients, I felt I could use this experience to develop an 'Emotional Processing Scale'. A simple, self-administered questionnaire could be a useful tool for emotion research and therapy.

Although it was ambitious to think it was possible to capture such an ephemeral phenomenon as emotions within a questionnaire, I thought it important to try.

In order to produce such an accurate measurement instrument two things were required: first, to develop an understanding or a 'model' of how emotional processing works and what are the key emotional dimensions involved, and second, to develop a way to measure each of these dimensions and produce a numerical scale.

It may seem strange to reduce emotions to numbers, but that does allow scientific study to proceed and knowledge to accumulate, even if it lacks the personal touch. Both parts of the equation would work together. Specifying the model would help in developing the measurement; and the gathering of data with that measurement instrument would further help to refine an understanding of the process.

It was at this point in 1993 that the project was put on ice as I moved jobs. This was not quite a John O'Groats to Land's End relocation but not far off; my family moved to Bournemouth on the south coast of England, where I was responsible for setting up a new research unit in mental health. With the many new tasks that the job demanded there was not much time to spend on emotion research, but the ideas kept ticking over in the background. During this time I continued to see patients for psychological therapy, not just for panic, but many other conditions too. Whenever patients said anything interesting about how they coped with emotional situations I would make a mental note of it. In my own life, if I was personally upset, hurt or stressed, I would observe in particular how the feelings of distress diminished, how long this took, whether such things as eating or drinking, doing other tasks, talking about it and so on affected the rate of decay of the feelings. Incidentally, this is a good way of translating personal hurts and distress into positive and valuable material. Perhaps there is a therapy somewhere in this! I kept a record of possible questions for a questionnaire. One summer holiday was spent writing seven draft chapters for this book, which I discarded when, on reading them through, I realized then that I did not know enough about emotions. It was back to the drawing board.

Over the next few years I tried to understand more about emotional processing using various sources, including scientific books and articles on emotions from clinical psychology and psychotherapy, psychoanalysis, neuropsychology, experimental psychology, philosophy, history and sociology; instances from films, newspapers and novels; a series of research interviews in 'phenomological' style with healthy individuals about their emotional life, conducted with Professor Les Todres at

163

Bournemouth University; and as before, what patients told me during psychological therapy. My list of possible items for a questionnaire grew longer.

Finally, at Christmas time on the eve of the new millennium, while walking on the banks of the River Stour in the snow, I concluded that the time seemed right to formally start devising an emotional processing questionnaire.

This emphasis on questionnaires probably seems an odd way to proceed, so I should take a few moments to explain this further. The area of psychology devoted to assessments, questionnaires, tests and psychological measurement scales is called psychometrics. It is a field of psychological science in its own right with its own set of principles and practices about the scientific development of questionnaires. For instance, the selection of questions should be based on a sound theory or body of evidence about what ought to be assessed. Plucking questions out of the air is not enough. A questionnaire will usually go through several metamorphoses. It is tried out on one group of individuals, then improved; tried again, improved; and so on, until a well-honed questionnaire is ready.

One key mathematical technique used in improving the questionnaire at each stage is called 'factor analysis'. There is a simple guideline on how many people should be tested out with the questionnaire, that is, ten individuals for each question in the questionnaire. For a questionnaire of fifty questions, 500 people are required, and so on. The reason so many people are needed is that the calculation rotates the scores (expressed in numbers) in dimensional space to discover separate groupings of questions. We are all familiar with three dimensions, but for a questionnaire with fifty questions the answers are initially rotated in fifty-dimensional space in order to produce the perfect separation between meanings! In modern statistical programs this seemingly impossible calculation is achieved in a millisecond. The researcher is left staring at tables of numbers, which indicate how many different meanings are contained in the questionnaire, and which questions belong to each meaning.

The factor analysis doesn't tell us what these meanings are – it simply presents scores and probabilities. It is then up to the human being, and researchers are mostly human beings, to determine *why* certain questions hang together. Are they concerned with memorizing the past, are they all 'happiness' items, do they all seem to express conflict, or what? The researcher often assigns a name to each factor, which in one word captures the inherent meaning or theme of the groups of questions. For instance, with the Emotional Processing Scale,[8] 'suppression' and 'avoidance' of emotions always came out clearly as separate factors. Although it may be hard to believe, factor analysis fascinates researchers through a sort of mysticism. Secret meanings, which cannot be determined by simply looking at questionnaire scores, can be discovered by a mathematical mystique.

The team grows

With each 'metamorphosis' of the questionnaire, new researchers began to join the team. Professor Peter Thomas, Professor of Healthcare Statistics and Epidemiology at Bournemouth University, brought real rigour into our research design and analysis; Dr Sarah Thomas, Senior Research Fellow, brought tremendous precision to the study by helping us to understand the many different types of factor analysis and helped to ground the research better in the experimental psychology literature. Research assistants Jane Holloway, Matthew Owen, Lara Tosunlar, Phil Gower and Anna Whittlesea, contributed intelligently and creatively to the research programme. Mariaelisa Santanastaso, a research psychologist at Bologna University working with Psychometrics Professor Paola Gremigni, who had conducted research with the Emotional Processing Scale in Italy, was able to add a new dimension to understanding the similarities and differences between English and Italian ways of coping with emotions. Each new study, with its new set of factor analyses, provided more information about the underlying structure of emotional processing. In each successive study we could modify questions to help pinpoint more clearly the nature of each emotional processing dimension, reaching towards a clearer understanding of the different elements and dynamics of emotional processing.

In 2000, our Research Unit moved from Bournemouth University to Poole General Hospital, where we worked closely with Dr Paul Thompson and Dr Selwyn Richards, both Consultant Rheumatologists involved in research and interested in the interaction of emotional factors and physical disease. This brought us into contact with patients suffering from chronic pain, fibromyalgia, back pain, chronic fatigue and rheumatic conditions, allowing us to discover that the principle I initially thought applied to panic sufferers applied equally well in chronic pain and fatigue. Not long after this new angle seemed to be crystallizing, Sharon Lothian, a trainee clinical psychologist, conducted her doctoral research thesis in emotional processing in patients with colorectal cancer. Although the scores of cancer patients differed from patients with psychological disorders, significant emotional processing effects were found distinguishing them from healthy people of the same age.

How far did this emotional processing extend, then? To panic, anxiety, depression, psychosomatic ailments and possibly cancer too? To help the project develop further we set up a website (www.emotionalprocessing.org.uk) in 2004, designed to bring all the different strands together. We asked many colleagues, clinicians and researchers to write chapters for us covering psychological disorders, psychosomatic conditions and physical disease. We had sections on chronic pain, cancer, chronic fatigue syndrome, old age, childbirth, autism and tears, crossing the boundaries between health and illness, from the journalistic to the seriously academic. Once we had launched the site we discovered many other clinicians and researchers who were also interested in emotional processing. We have steadily built up a group of research collaborators around the world studying emotional processing in topics as diverse as headaches to music therapy. The Emotional Processing Scale has been translated into Italian, Hindi, Danish, Japanese and French, and we are regularly surprised at some new application. The Italian research psychologist Mariaelisa Santanastaso is currently drawing these strands together into a PhD on 'Cross-cultural Comparison of Emotional Processing'. Soon we really will be in a position to test whether the British 'stiff upper lip' is fact or fiction.

References

Chapter 1

1. Freud, S., 'On the Grounds for Detaching a Particular Syndrome from Neurasthenia under the Description "Anxiety Neurosis"' (1894), in J. Strachey (ed.), *The Standard Edition of the Complete Works of Sigmund Freud*, Vol. III, London: Hogarth, 1962.
2. Vose, R.H., *Agoraphobia*, London: Faber and Faber, 1981.

Chapter 2

1. Frey, W.H. and Langseth, M., *Crying: The Mystery of Tears*, Minneapolis: Winston, 1985.
2. Hastrup, J.L., Baker, J.G., Kraemer, D.L. et al., 'Crying and Depression Among Older Adults', *The Gerontologist*, 26, 1986, pp. 91–96.
3. Porter, R., *The Greatest Benefit to Mankind: A Medical History from Antiquity to the Present*, London: Fontana Press, 1997.
4. Darwin, C., *The Expression of the Emotions in Man and Animals* (1872), ed. P. Ekman, London: Harper Collins, 1998.
5. MacLean, P.D., 'Some Psychiatric Implications of Physiological Studies on the Frontotemporal Portion of Limbic System (visceral brain)', *Electroencephalography and Clinical Neurophysiology*, 4, 1952, pp. 407–18.
6. MacLean, P.D., 'Psychosomatic Disease and the "Visceral Brain": Recent Development Bearing on Papez Theory of Emotion', *Psychosomatic Medicine*, 11, 1949, pp. 338–53.
7. MacLean, P.D., *The Triune Brain in Evolution: Role in Paleocerebral Functions*, New York: Plenum Press, 1990.
8. Le Doux, J.E., 'Emotion and the Limbic System Concept', *Concepts in Neuroscience*, 2, 1991, pp. 169–99.
9. Le Doux, J.E., *The Emotional Brain: The Mysterious Underpinnings of Emotional Life*, New York: Touchstone, 1996.
10. Damasio, A., *Descartes' Error: Emotion, Reason and the Human Brain*, New York: Grosset/Putnam, 1994.
11. Goleman, D., *Emotional Intelligence: Why It Can Matter More Than IQ*, New York: Bantam Books, 1995.
12. Lazarus, R.S., *Stress and Emotion: A New Synthesis*, London: Free Association Books, 1999.
13. Damasio, A., see above, note 10.
14. Le Doux, J.E., see above, note 9.

Chapter 3

1. Epstein, S., 'Emotions and Psychopathology from the Perspective of Cognitive-Experiential Self Theory', in W.F. Flack and J.D. Laird (eds), *Emotion in Psychopathology*, New York: Oxford University Press, 1988.
2. Bucci, W., *Psychoanalysis and Cognitive Science: A Multiple Code Theory*, New York: Guildford Press, 1997.
3. De Casper, A. and Fifer, W., 'Of Human Bonding: Newborns Prefer Their Mother's Voices', *Science*, 208, 1980, p. 1174.
4. Krystal, H., *Integration and Self-healing: Affect, Trauma, Alexythymia*, New Jersey: Analytic Press, 1988.
5. Bowlby, J.C., *Attachment and Loss*, New York: Basic Books, 1967.
6. Gerhardt, S., *Why Love Matters: How Affection Shapes a Baby's Brain*, London: Routledge, 2004.
7. Beebe, B. and Lachman, F.M., 'The Contribution of Mother–Infant Mutual Influence to the Origins of Self- and Object-Representations', *Psychoanalytic Psychology*, 5, 1988, pp. 305–37.
8. Mahler, M.S., Pine, F. and Bergman, A., *The Psychological Birth of the Human Infant: Symbiosis and Individuation*, New York: Basic Books, 1975.
9. Blum, H., 'Separation-Individuation and Attachment Theory', *Journal of American Psychoanalytic Association*, 52, 2001, pp. 535–54.
10. Epstein, S., 'The Self-Concept Revisited, or a Theory of Theory', *American Psychologist*, 28, 1983, pp. 404–16.

Chapter 4

1. Bucci, W., 'Pathways of Emotional Communication', *Psychoanalytic Enquiry*, 21, 2001, p. 40.
2. Gendlin, E., *Focusing*, 2nd Edition, New York: Bantam Books, 1981.
3. Rogers, C., *On Becoming a Person: A Therapist's View of Psychotherapy*, London: Constable, 1961.
4. Mahler, M.S., Pine, F. and Bergman, A., *The Psychological Birth of the Human Infant: Symbiosis and Individuation*, New York: Basic Books, 1975.
5. Paivio, S.C. and Greenberg, L.S., 'Experiential Theory of Emotions Applied to Anxiety and Depression', in W.F. Flack and J.D. Laird (eds), *Emotion in Psychopathology*, New York: Oxford University Press, 1998.

Chapter 5

1. Rachman, J., 'Emotional Processing', *Behaviour Research and Therapy*, 18, 1980, pp. 51–60.
2. Baker, R., Thomas, S., Thomas, P.W. and Owens, M., 'Development of an Emotional Processing Scale', *Journal of Psychosomatic Research*, 62, 2007, pp. 167–78.
3. Wagner, V., Gaise, S., Haider, H. *et al.*, 'Sleep Inspires Insight', *Nature*, 427, 2004, pp. 352–55.
4. Maquet, P., 'The Role of Sleep in Learning and Memory', *Science*, 294, 2001, 1048–82.
5. Baker, R., Allen, H., Gibson, S. *et al.*, 'Evaluation of Primary Care Counselling in Dorset', *British Journal of General Practice*, 48, 1998, pp. 1049–53.
6. Baker, R., Baker, E., Allen, H. *et al.*, 'A Naturalistic Longitudinal Evaluation of Counselling in Primary Care', *Counselling Psychology Quarterly*, 15, 2002, pp. 359–73.

Chapter 6

1. Baker, R., 'An Emotional Processing Model for Counselling and Psychotherapy: A Way Forward?', *Counselling in Practice*, 7 (1), 2001, pp. 8–11.
2. Baker, R., 'Model of Emotional Processing', 2004. This can be found at: www.emotionalprocessing.org.uk
3. Rachman, S., 'Emotional Processing', *Behaviour Research and Therapy*, 18, 1980, pp. 51–60.
4. Foa, E.B. and Kozak, M.J., 'Emotional Processing of Fear: Exposure to Corrective Information', *Psychological Bulletin*, 99, 1986, pp. 20–35.
5. Armony, J.L. and Le Doux, J.E., 'How the Brain Processes Emotional Information', *Annual New York Academy of Science*, 821, 1997, pp. 259–70.
6. Ortony, A., Collins, A. and Clore, G.L., *The Cognitive Structure of Emotions*, Cambridge: Cambridge University Press, 1988.
7. Oatley, K. and Duncan, D., 'The Experience of Emotions in Everyday Life', *Cognition and Emotion*, 8, 1994, pp. 369–81.
8. Beck, A.T., *Cognitive Therapy and the Emotional Disorders*, New York: International University Press, 1976.
9. Mogg, K. and Bradley, B.P., 'A Cognitive-Motivational Analysis of Anxiety', *Behaviour Research and Therapy*, 36, 1998, pp. 809–48.
10. Gendlin, E.T., *Focusing-Oriented Psychotherapy: A Manual of the Experiential Method*, New York: Guildford, 1996.
11. Rogers, Carl, R., 'To Be That Self Which One Truly Is' in *A Therapist's View of Psychotherapy: On Becoming a Person*, London: Constable, 1961.
12. Greenberg, L., Rice, L. and Eliot, R., *Facilitating Emotional Change: The Moment by Moment Process*, New York: Guildford, 1993.
13. Brosschot, J.F. and Aarsse, H.R., 'Restrictive Emotional Processing and Somatic Attribution in Fibromyalgia', *International Journal of Psychiatry in Medicine*, 31, 2001, pp. 127–46.
14. Kennedy-Moore, E. and Watson, J.C., *Expressing Emotion*, New York: Guildford Press, 1999.
15. Scheff, T.J., *Catharsis in Healing, Ritual and Drama*, Berkeley University and California Press, 1979.
16. Bohart, A.C., 'Towards a Cognitive Theory of Catharsis', *Psychotherapy: Theory, Research and Practice*, 17, 1980, pp. 192–201.
17. Pennebaker, J.W., *Opening Up: The Healing Power of Expressing Emotions*, New York: Guildford Press, 1997.
18. Richards, J.M. and Gross, J.J., 'Emotion Regulation and Memory: The Cognition Costs of Keeping One's Cool', *Journal of Personality and Social Psychology*, 79, 2000, pp. 410–24.
19. Whelton, W.J., 'Emotional Processes in Psychotherapy: Evidence Across Therapeutic Modalities', *Clinical Psychology and Psychotherapy*, 11, 2004, pp. 58–71.
20. Gross, J.J., and Thompson, R.A.P., 'Emotion Regulation, Conceptual Foundations', in J.J. Gross (ed.), *Handbook of Emotion Regulation*, New York: Guildford Press, 2007.
21. Salters-Pedneault, K., Tul, M.T., Roemer, L., 'The Role of Avoidance of Emotional Material in the Anxiety Disorders', *Applied and Preventative Psychology*, 11, 2004, pp. 95–114.

Chapter 7

1. Leonard, N.E., *The Locomotive God*, London: Chapman and Hall, 1928.
2. Wolpe, J., *Psychotherapy by Reciprocal Inhibition*, Stamford: Stamford University Press, 1958.
3. Krapff, J.E. and Nawas, M., 'Differential Orders of Stimulus Presentation in Systematic Desensitisation', *Journal of Abnormal Psychology*, 75, 1970, p. 333.
4. Stein, R. and Marks, I., 'Brief and Prolonged Flooding: A Comparison in Agoraphobic Patients', *Archives of General Psychiatry*, 28, 1973, p. 270.
5. Emmekamp, P.M.G. and Wessels, H., 'Flooding in Imagination vs Flooding In Vivo: A Comparison with Agoraphobics', *Behaviour Research and Therapy*, 13, 1975, p. 7.

6. Gillam, P. and Rachman, S., 'An Experimental Investigation of Behaviour Therapy in Phobic Patients', *British Journal of Psychiatry*, 124, 1974, p. 392.

7. Marks, I.M., 'Exposure Treatments: Conceptual Issues', in *Behaviour Modification: Principles and Clinical Applications* (2nd edition), W.S. Agras (ed.), Boston: Little, Brown and Co, 1978.

8. Marks, I.M., 'Exposure Treatments: Clinical Applications', in *Behaviour Modification: Principles and Clinical Applications* (2nd edition), W.S. Agras (ed.), Boston: Little, Brown and Co, 1978.

9. Eysenck, H.J., 'The Conditioning Model of Neurosis', *Behaviour and Brain Science*, 2, 1979, pp. 155–99.

10. Foa, E.B., Steketee, G. and Grayson, J.B., 'Imaginal and In Vivo Exposure: A Comparison with Obsessive Compulsive Checkers', *Behaviour Therapy* 16, 1985, pp. 292–302.

11. Ramsay, R.W., 'Behaviour Approaches to Bereavement', *Behaviour Research and Therapy*, 5, 1977, pp. 131–35.

12. Blakey, R. and Baker, R., 'An Exposure Approach to Alcohol Abuse', *Behaviour Research and Therapy*, 18, 1980, pp. 319–25.

Chapter 8

1. *DSM III, Diagnostic and Statistical Manual of Mental Disorders*, 3rd edition, Washington: American Psychiatric Association, 1980.

2. Horowitz, M.J., Wilner, N., Caltreider, N. et al., 'Signs and Symptoms of Post-Traumatic Stress Disorder', *Archives of General Psychiatry*, 140, 1980, pp. 1543–50.

3. Foa, E.B. and Meadows, E.A., 'Psychosocial Treatments for Post-Traumatic Stress Disorder: A Critical Review', *Annual Review of Psychology*, 48, 1997.

4. Foa, E.B. and Rothbaum, B.O., *Treating the Trauma of Rape: Cognitive-Behavioural Therapy for PTSD*, New York: Guildford, 1998.

5. Jayco, L.H., Foa, E.B. and Morral, A.R., 'Predicting Response to Exposure Treatment in PTSD: The Role of Mental Deficit and Alienation', *Journal of Consulting and Clinical Psychology*, 66, 1998, pp. 185–92.

6. Rachman, S., 'Emotional Processing, with Special Reference to Post Traumatic Stress Disorder', *International Review of Psychiatry*, 13, 2001, pp. 164-71.

7. Foa, E.B. and Kozak, M.J., 'Emotional Processing in Fear: Exposure to Corrective Information', *Psychological Bulletin*, 97, 1986, pp. 20–35.

Chapter 9

1. Allport, G.W., *The Use of Psychological Documents in Psychological Science*, New York: Social Science Research Council, 1951.

2. Freud, S., *Selected Papers on Hysteria and Other Psychoneuroses* (1909), No.4 of the Neurosis and Mental Disease Monograph Series, New York.

3. Lutz, T., *Crying: The Natural and Cultural History of Tears*, New York: Norton, 1999.

Chapter 10

1. Darwin, C., *The Expression of the Emotions in Man and Animals* (1872), ed. P. Ekman, London: Harper Collins, 1998.

2. Ekman, P., Friesen, W.V. and Ellsworth, P., 'What Emotions Categories or Dimensions Can Observers Judge from Facial Behaviour?' in P. Ekman (ed.), *Emotion in the Human Face*, New York: Cambridge University Press, 1982.

3. Ortony, A. and Turner, T.J., 'What's Basic About Basic Emotions?', *Psychological Review*, 97, 1990, pp. 315–31.

4. Wierzbicka, A., 'Human Emotions: Universal or Culture Specific?', *American Anthropologist*, 88, 1986, pp. 584–94.

5. Mesquita, B., 'Culture and Emotions: Different Approaches to the Question', Chapter 7 in *Emotions: Current Issues and Future Directions*, eds T.J. Maynes and G.A. Bonanno, New York: Guildford Press, 2001.

6. Capsi, A., Elder, G.H. and Bem, D.J., 'Moving Against the World: Life Course Patterns of Explosive Children', *Developmental Psychology*, 23, 1987, pp. 308–13.

7. Olweus, D., 'Stability of Aggressive Reaction Patterns in Males: A Review', *Psychological Bulletin*, 86, 1979, pp. 852–75.

8. Rubin, K.H., 'The Waterloo Longitudinal Project: Correlates and Consequences of Social Withdrawal from Childhood to Adolescence', in K.H. Rubin and J. Asendorpf (eds), *Social Withdrawal, Inhibition and Shyness in Childhood*, Hillsdale, NJ: Erlbaum, 1993.

9. Harrington, R., Fudge, H., Rutter, M. et al., 'Adult Outcomes of Childhood and Adolescent Depression', *Archives of General Psychiatry*, 47, 1990, pp. 1112–17.

10. Young, J.E. and Klosko, J.S., *Reinventing Your Life: How to Break Free from Negative Life Patterns*, New York: Penguin Group, 1994.

11. Bucci, W., *Psychoanalysis and Cognitive Science: A Multiple Code Theory*, New York: Guildford Press, 1997.

12. Jenkins, J.M. and Oatley, K., 'Emotion Schemas in Children', Chapter 3 of W.F. Flack and J.D. Laird (eds), *Emotions in Psychopathology*, Oxford: OUP, 1998.

Chapter 11

1. DeRijk, R., Michelson, D., Karp, B. *et al.*, 'Exercise and Circadian Rhythm-Induced Variations in Plasma Cortisol Differentially Regulate Interleukin-1 beta (IL-1 beta), I-6 and Tumour Necrosis Factor-alpha (TNF-alpha) Production in Humans: High Sensitivity of TNF-alpha and Resistance of IL-6', *Journal of Clinical Endocrinology and Metabolism*, 82, 1997, pp. 2182–92.

2. Keicolt-Glaser, J.K., Page, G.G., Marucha, P.T. *et al.*, 'Psychological Influences on Surgical Recovery: Perspectives from Psychoneuroimmunology', *American Psychologist*, 53, 1998, pp. 1209–18.

3. Glaser, R., Sheridan, J.F., Malarkey, W.B. *et al.*, 'Chronic Stress Modulates the Immune Response to a Pneumococcal Vaccine', *Psychosomatic Medicine*, 62, 2000, pp. 804–07.

4. Malarkey, W.B., Wu, H., Cacioppo, I.T. *et al.*, 'Chronic Stress Down Regulates Growth Hormone Gene Expression in Peripheral Blood Mononuclear Cells of Older Adults', *Endocrine*, 5, 1996, pp. 33–39.

5. Dimitroglon, E., Zafiropoulon, Messini-Nikolaki, N., Dondonnakis, S. *et al.*, 'DNA Damage in a Human Population Affected by Chronic Psychogenic Stress', *International Journal of Hygiene and Environmental Health*, 206, 1, 2003, pp. 39–44.

6. Cohen, L., Marshall, G.D., Cheng, L. *et al.*, 'DNA Repair Capacity in Healthy Medical Students During and After Exam Stress', *Journal of Behavioural Medicine*, 23, 2000, pp. 531–44.

7. Mayne, T., 'Negative Affect and Health: The Importance of Being Earnest', *Cognition and Emotion*, 13, 2000, pp. 601–35.

8. Manuck, S.B., Marsland, A.L., Kaplan, J.R. *et al.*, 'The Pathogenicity of Behaviour and its Neuroendocrine Mediation: An Example from Coronary Artery Disease', *Psychosomatic Medicine* 57, 1995, pp. 215–28.

9. Sapolsky, R.M., *Why Zebras Don't Get Ulcers: A Guide to Stress, Stress-related Diseases and Coping*, New York: Freeman, 1974.

10. Glaser, R. and Kiecolt-Glaser, J. (eds), *Handbook of Human Stress and Immunity*, San Diego: Academic, 1994.

11. Mayne, T.J., 'Emotions and Health', Chapter 12 in *Emotions, Current Issues and Future Predictions*, eds T.J. Mayne and G.A. Bonanno, New York: Guildford Press, 2001.

12. Kiecolt-Glaser, J.K., McGuire, L., Robles, T.F. *et al.*, 'Emotions, Morbidity and Mortality: New Perspectives from Psychoneuroimmunology', *Annual Review of Psychology*, 53, 2002, pp. 83–107.

13. Mayne, T.J., see above, note 11.

14. Peveler, R., Kilkenny, L. and Kinmonth, A-M., 'Medically Unexplained Physical Symptoms in Primary Care: A Comparison of Self-Report Questionnaires and Clinical Opinion', *Journal of Psychosomatic Research* 42, 1997, pp. 253–60.

15. Munk-Jorgensen, P., 'Somatization in Primary Care: Prevalence, Health Care Utilization, and General Practitioner Recognition', *Psychosomatics*, 40, 1999, pp. 330–38.

16. Reid, S., Wessely, S., Crayford, T. *et al.*, 'Medically Unexplained Symptoms in Frequent Attenders of Secondary Health Care: Retrospective Cohort Study', *British Medical Journal*, 322, 2001, pp. 767–69.

17. McCormack, J., 'Medically Unexplained Symptoms in Secondary Care', *British Medical Journal*, 323, 2001, p. 397.

18. Spurr, J., 'Emotional Processing and Physical Health: Somatization'. This can be found at: www.emotionalprocessing.org.uk

Chapter 12

1. Rimé, B., Philippot, P., Boca, S. *et al.*, 'Long-Lasting Consequence of Emotion: Social Sharing and Rumination', in W. Shoebe and M. Henstone (eds), *European Review of Social Psychology*, Chichester: Wiley, 1992.

2. Philippot, P. and Rimé, B., 'Social and Cognitive Processing in Emotion', Chapter 8 of W.F. Flack and J.D. Laird (eds), *Emotions in Psychopathology*, Oxford: Oxford University Press, 1998.

3. Foa, E.B. and Kozak, M.J., 'Emotional Processing in Fear: Exposure to Corrective Information', *Psychological Bulletin*, 97, 1986, pp. 20–35.

4. Bucci, W., *Psychoanalysis and Cognitive Science: A Multiple Code Theory*, New York: Guildford Press, 1997.

5. McCullough, M.E., Bellah, C.G., Kilpatrick, S.D. *et al.*, 'Vengefulness: Relationship with Forgiveness, Rumination, Well-Being and the Big Five', *Personality and Social Psychology Bulletin*, 27, 2001, pp. 601–10.

6. Baker, R., *Understanding Panic Attacks and Overcoming Fear*, Oxford: Lion Publishing, 2003.

7. Ingram, R.E., 'Self-Focused Attention in Clinical Disorders: Review and a Conceptual Model', *Psychological Bulletin*, 107, 1990, pp. 156–76.

8. Barsky, A.J., 'Amplification, Somatizaton and the Somatoform Disorders', *Psychosomatics*, 39, 1992, pp. 28–34.

9. Scholtz, O.B., Ott, R. and Sarnoch, H., 'Proprioception in Somatoform Disorders', *Behaviour Research and Therapy*, 39, 2001, pp. 1429–38.

10. Sharp, T.J., 'Chronic Pain: A Reformulation of the Cognitive-Behavioural Model', *Behaviour Research and Therapy*, 39, 2001, pp. 787–800.

Chapter 13

1. Tarvis, C., 'On the Wisdom of Counting to Ten: Personal and Social Dangers of Anger Expression', in P. Shaver (ed.) *Reviewing Personality and Social Psychology*, Vol 5, Beverley Hills: Sage, 1984.

2. Miller, T.Q., Smith, T.W., Turner, C.W. et al., 'A Meta-analytic Review of Research on Hostility and Physical Health', *Psychological Bulletin*, 119, 1996, pp. 322–48.

3. Everson, S.A., Kauhanen, J., Kaplan, G.A. et al., 'Hostility and Increased Risk of Mortality and Acute Myocardial Infarction: The Mediating Role of Behavioural Risk Factors', *American Journal of Epidemiology*, 146, 1997, pp. 142–52.

4. Vahtera, J., Kivimaki, M., Koskenvuo, M. et al., 'Hostility and Registered Sickness Absences: A Prospective Study of Municipal Employees', *Psychological Medicine*, 27, 1997, pp. 693–701.

5. Obrist, P.A., *Cardiovascular Psychophysiology: A Perspective*, New York: Pergamon Press, 1981.

6. Pratt, L.A., Ford, D.E., Crum, R.M. et al., 'Depression, Psychotropic Medication, and Risk of Myocardial Infarction', *Circulation*, 94, 1996, pp. 3123–29.

7. Glassman, A.H. and Shapiro, P.A., 'Depression and the Course of Coronary Artery Disease', *American Journal of Psychiatry*, 155, 1998, pp. 4–11.

8. Penninx, B.W.J.H., Guralnik, J.M., Pahor, M. et al., 'Chronically Depressed Mood and Cancer Risk in Older Persons', *Journal of National Cancer Institute*, 90, 1998, pp. 1888–93.

9. Michelson, D., Stratakis, C., Hill, L. et al., 'Bone Mineral Density in Women with Depression', *New England Journal of Medicine*, 335, 1996, pp. 1176–81.

10. Rantanen, T., Penninx, B.W.J.H., Masaki, K. et al., 'Depressed Mood and Body Mass Index as Predictors of Muscle Strength Decline in Older Men', *Journal of American Geriatric Society*, 48, 2000, pp. 613–17.

11. Grossarth-Maticek, R., Bastiaans, J. and Kanazir, D., 'Psychosocial Factors as Strong Predictors of Mortality from Cancer, Ischaemic Heart Disease and Stroke: The Yugoslav Prospective Study', *Personality and Individual Differences*, 29, 1985, pp. 167–76.

12. Gross, J.J. and Thompson, R.A.P., 'Emotion Regulation: Conceptual Foundations', in J.J. Gross (ed.), *Handbook of Emotion Regulation*, New York: Guildford Press, 2007.

13. Oshner, K.N. and Gross, J.J., 'The Cognitive Control of Emotion', *Trends in Cognitive Science*, 9, 2005, pp. 242–49.

14. Salters-Redneault, K., Tull, M.T. and Roemer, L., 'The Role of Avoidance of Emotional Material in Anxiety Disorders', *Applied and Preventative Psychology*, 11, 2004, pp. 95–114.

15. Wegner, D.M., 'Ironic Processes of Mental Control', *Psychological Review*, 101, 1998, pp. 34–52.

16. Wegner, D.M., Schneider, D. J., Carter, S.R. et al., 'Paradoxical Effects of Thought Suppression', *Journal of Personality and Social Psychology*, 53, 1987, pp. 5–13.

17. Rogers. C., *On Becoming a Person: A Therapist's View of Psychotherapy*, London: Constable, 1961.

Appendix

1. Baker, R., *Understanding Panic Attacks and Overcoming Fear*, Oxford: Lion Publishing, 2003.

2. Faravelli, J.A., 'Life Events Preceding the Onset of Panic Disorder', *Journal of Affective Disorders*, 9, 1985, pp. 103–05.

3. Kleiner, L. and Marshall, W.L., 'The Role of Interpersonal Problems in the Development of Agoraphobia with Panic Attacks', *Journal of Anxiety Disorders*, 1, 1987, pp. 313–23.

4. Baker, R., 'Personal Accounts of Panic', Chapter 5 in Baker, R. (ed.), *Panic Disorder: Theory, Research and Therapy*, Chichester: John Wiley, 1989.

5. Baker, R., Holloway, J., Thomas, P. W. et al., 'Emotional Processing and Panic', *Behaviour Research and Therapy*, 42, 2004, pp. 1271–87.

6. Pettingale, K.W., Watson, M. and Greer, S., 'The Validity of Emotional Control as a Trait in Breast Cancer Patients', *Journal of Psychosocial Oncology*, 2, 1984, pp. 21–30.

7. Baker, R. and Hall, J.N., 'REHAB: A New Assessment Instrument for Chronic Psychiatric Patients', *Schizophrenia Bulletin*, 14, 1988, pp. 97–111.

8. Baker, R., Thomas, S., Thomas, P.W. and Owens, M., 'Development of an Emotional Processing Scale', *Journal of Psychosomatic Research*, 62, 2007, pp. 167–78.

Index

A

abreaction 103
accepting emotions 82, 99, 100, 104, 152–53, 157
affect 51, 102
affect-laden memory 93, 102, 103, 137–38
aggression 113–15, 145–46
agoraphobia 77, 160
alcoholism 53, 54, 75, 76, 81
amygdala 23
anger 62, 63–64, 112, 115, 124, 135, 147, 149, 155–56
animals and emotion 39
anxiety 12, 13,112, 118, 135, 142–43, 160–61
appraisal
    and schemas 117–19
    of the meaning of events 61, 62, 156
    of motives of others 156–57
assertiveness training 149
attachment 33–34
avoiding emotional pain 152
awareness of emotion 41, 42, 63, 64, 146, 148

B

balance in emotions 149–50
'basic emotions' 110, 111
Beck, Aaron
    and cognitive therapy 115, 160
behavioural exposure 79, 80, 81, 89, 104, 157
behaviour therapy 75–76, 78, 82
bereavement see 'grief'
bitterness 132–34
    see also 'anger'
blocked emotion 9, 10, 54, 70, 71, 101, 125
blocked memories 71, 87, 124
blushing 96, 152
bonding 33–34
bottling up emotions 11–14, 101–02
Bowlby, John
    and attachment theory 33
brain 22–26, 127
Bucci, Wilma 29, 38, 116
    and emotion schemas 115–16
    and Multiple Code Theory 29, 30, 116
    and sub-symbolic images 29, 116
    and 'the good therapist' 38–39

C

cancer 148, 161, 166
catharsis 101, 102–04
changing emotions 149–53, 156–57
childhood experience 7, 8, 53, 54, 77
cognition and emotion 24–25
cognitive appraisal 61, 62, 156–57
compassionate appraisals 156–57
conditioning 78–80
confusion 125–26
controlling emotions
    control of experience of emotions 70, 71, 151–53, 161
    control of expression of emotions 71, 161
    control of input of emotions 70, 150–51
    helpful control 97, 150
    unhelpful control 97, 150, 161
counselling
    effectiveness of 96
    versus debriefing 136–37
cortex 23–25
crying 9, 10, 21, 95, 96, 103, 115, 142, 160
culture
    and 'basic emotions' 110–12
    and emotion rulebooks 108–10
    and expressing emotions 112, 167

D

Damasio, Antonio
    and role of the cortex in emotions 23, 24
Darwin, Charles
    and 'basic emotions' 110
    and emotional expression 21, 22
    and evolutionary theory 110
decision-making and emotion 24
denying emotions 124–25
depression 8–10, 143, 146, 148, 161
development of emotions in children 30, 31, 34–36, 54, 64
disgust 111, 140
dissociation 70, 71
DNA and emotions see 'genetics and emotion'
dreams 53

E

emotion
    allowing enjoyment 47
    allowing reality to be experienced 44–45

as conveying information   39, 40, 41
as energy   14, 104
as hard-wired   24–25
as sin   19, 20
blocked   9, 10, 70, 71, 124, 130, 148
elements of   58–71
giving and receiving love   47
grounded in the body   41–42, 60, 112, 135
in experiencing beauty   43, 44
integrated with thinking   35, 36
interpersonal nature   28, 29
intuition   39–40
language   22, 23, 30, 31, 111
model   58–71
part of humanity   47, 158
preceding thought   42
purpose of   41, 44, 45, 47
regulation   70, 150
relating to self   34–35, 46, 47
rulebooks   108, 109
schemas   115–18, 138, 142, 156–57
transcendent nature   44
emotional dissociation   70, 71
emotional inhibition   9, 10, 70, 148
Emotional Intelligence   24
emotional lability   139
emotional over-responsiveness   139
emotional pain   99, 100, 121, 122
emotional processing
    appraisal of emotions   61, 62, 117–19, 150, 153–56
    as an immune system   51, 52, 157
    assessment   101, 161–67
    blockages in   53, 54, 10, 11, 157
    definition   51
    experiencing emotions   62, 63, 99, 100, 139–42, 151–53
    expressing emotions   65–67, 146, 148
    nature of   51, 52, 82, 102, 103, 104–05, 139–42, 157
    registering emotions   61, 62, 117–18, 136
    therapy   10, 91–92, 94, 124–26, 142, 157
emotional processing scale   161–63, 164–67
emotional regulation   70, 150
emotional release   101–02, 104, 146–47
emotional suppression   11, 13, 56, 57, 70, 98
Epstein, Seymour
    and emotion and reason   29

experiencing emotions   62, 63, 99, 100
    as gestalt   63, 64
    awareness   41–42, 63
    different from expressing   71, 149
    labelling   41–42, 63, 64, 148
    linking   41–42, 63, 64, 148
exposure therapy   80, 81, 89, 104, 157
expressing emotion   65–67, 146, 148
extrasensory perception   37–40

F

facing emotions   82, 99, 100, 104, 152–53, 154, 157
falling in love   *see* 'love'
fatigue   124, 166
fear   59, 78, 143
fibromyalgia   121, 126, 166
Foa, Edna   80
    and emotional processing and trauma   88, 140, 141
focusing   41
forgetting   56, 57
forgiveness   142, 149
Freud, Sigmund   12
    and abreaction   103
    and anxiety   12
    and catharsis   102, 103, 104
    and cathartic method   55
    and hydraulic theory   13
    and memory   102, 103
    and sexual theory   12, 13
    and talking therapy   55

G

gender and emotion   20, 21, 112
Gendlin, Eugene
    and focusing   41
genetics and emotion   110–13, 127
God, as pure reason   19
Goleman, Daniel
    and *Emotional Intelligence*   24, 25
grief   10, 56, 57, 80, 97, 124, 132–33, 146
Gross, James
    and emotion regulation   70, 150
guilt   10, 111, 142

H

habituation   82, 104
happiness   47, 151–53
'healing through feeling'   83, 104, 157, 151–53
health and emotions   13–14, 121–23, 126–28, 130, 147–49, 161, 166

heart   127, 143, 147, 148, 160
hostility   *see* 'anger'
hyperarousal   87

I

illness and emotions   *see* 'health and emotions'
incubation effect   61, 117–19
input event   61, 117–19, 136
immune systems, emotional and physical   50, 52, 157
integration of thought and emotion   25, 35, 36
intuition   39–40

J

jealousy   112
Jesus
   as experiencing emotions   19–20

L

labelling emotion   41–42, 63, 64, 148
language and emotions   22, 23, 30, 31, 111
Le Doux, Joseph
   and limbic system   23, 25, 26
'life-traps'   *see* 'schema, emotion'
limbic system   23
linking emotion with events   6, 41–42, 63, 148
love   31–36, 47

M

Maclean, Paul
   and paleo-mammalian brain   22, 23
Mahler, Margaret
   and psychological birth of infant   34, 35, 46
Marks, Isaac   79
   and behavioural exposure   79, 80, 104
   and treatment of phobias   80
meaning in emotion   28, 63, 111, 112
measuring emotional processing   161–67
medically unexplained symptoms   127, 128
memory
   affect-laden   93, 94, 99, 102, 103, 137–38
   problems   87, 93–94, 124
   related to self   99, 115
   role in emotional processing   102, 103, 115
   traumatic   54, 56–57, 93, 94, 99
mood   139
mother–child relationship   33–35

N

negative emotions   47, 113, 119, 127
NHS, somatic focus of   121, 126–27
numbing of emotions   70, 71, 87

O

object relations   33–34
obsessions   80, 81
Origen   18–20

P

pain, physical   121, 122, 143
panic attacks   143, 160
phobias   22, 70, 77–80
positive emotions   47, 113, 115, 127
post-traumatic stress disorder   77, 86–87, 88, 89, 93, 96, 99, 134, 154
primal scream   101
'primitive' emotion brain   22, 23, 25
psychoanalysis   12–13, 55
psychosomatic   120–22, 130, 131, 166
psychotherapy
   difference with rumination   141
   difference with social sharing   105, 141
   origin   54–55

R

Rachman, Jack
   and definition of emotional processing   14, 51
reason and emotion   25, 29, 148
registering emotions   61, 62, 117–18, 136
rejection   35, 124
release of emotional feelings   101, 102–04, 146–47
resolution   10, 91–92, 94, 126, 157
revenge   135, 138–39, 142
Rimé, Bernard
   and rumination   137, 139
Rogers, Carl
   and emotional experience   26, 45, 153
   and person-centred therapy   45
rumination   135, 136, 139–44
ruminative cycle   140

S

sadness   8–10, 115, 142, 148
schema, emotion   115–19, 138, 142 , 156–58,
self   34–35, 46, 47
self-blame   142
self-depreciation   118
sensitization   89, 92

shame 111
shell shock 84–86
sleep 52–53
social sharing, difference with therapy 103–05, 141
somatic focus 64, 121, 123, 130, 131, 148
'stiff upper lip' 11, 109, 167
Stoics 19–20
storing up emotion 11–14, 101–02
stress 127, 139, 150–51
suppression 11, 13, 56–57, 97, 98, 157, 161

T
talking therapy 38–40, 55, 103–04, 141, 159
tears see 'crying'
temptation 19
therapy 41, 55, 78–80, 146
  difference with social sharing 103

thinking and emotion 24, 25, 35, 36
trauma, effects of 86, 87, 88, 93, 136, 137

U
understanding emotions 41, 42, 63, 64, 105, 148

V
verbal and non-verbal clues 39
verbal and non-verbal code 29–31, 116
vicious cycles 143

W
well-being and emotion see 'health and emotion'

Y
Young, Jeffrey
  and schemas/life-traps 115-16, 117, 118